CONFESSIONS
OF AN AGEING
TENNIS PLAYER

NICK OWEN

The must-go-to guide book for all of us who have never quite managed to succeed on the tennis court: or indeed anywhere else in life.

Remember when you were young and you emulated your sporting heroes in the streets or school playground? Remember the days when you were going to win the 100m sprint? The World Cup? Wimbledon? 'Confessions of an Ageing Tennis Player is a short story about our dreams and our disappointments, our failures and our triumphs.

It's about a man of a certain age who lived those fantasies when he was young and never quite moved on as he grew up. It's a story of how he becomes sporting zero to hero and back again set against the backdrop of Wimbledon in 2013 when Andy Murray was the first British player to win there in decades.

Unsurprisingly, Andy makes surprise appearances throughout the book.

Published by Nick Owen Publishing, Lincoln, UK.
Nick Owen Publishing Ltd is registered in England and Wales as a Company Limited by Guarantee (09435925).

Email   nick@nickowenpublishing.co.uk
Web   nickowenpublishing.wordpress.com
Twitter   @NickPublishing

ISBN   9798346119678

British Library Cataloguing in Publication Data.
A catalogue record for this book is available from the British Library.

Published 30 November 2021

ACKNOWLEDGEMENTS:
THANKS TO OUR CLUB APPRECIATORS GROUP.

Many thanks to everyone who helped support this book along its way:

Adrian Waite, Alby James, Anand Torrents, Andy Dawson, Andy Milne, Andy Warren, Anna-Karin Tobiassen, Anthony Haddon, Ben Barker, Beth Sheldrake, Billie Deen Owen, Bisakha Sarker, Brian Loughrey, Camilla Lokvik, Candace Lott, Christine Walters, Colin Aldred, David Cripps, David Llewellyn, David Manley, David Merino, David Robertson, Deana Wildgoose, Deborah Robinson, Derry Hunter, Elaine Harris, Fabio Orlandi, Gavin Cross, Gerry Murphy, Graeme Warren, Heidi Kammerer-Müller, Hope London, Jackie P. Gardner, Jackie Harrison, Claudette Howell, Jack Sutton, Jane McGinnes, Janice Owen, Janice Wilson, Jason Biggs, Jessie Antonellis John, Jo Carter, Jo Loyn, Jojo, John Quinn, Jon Stockdale, Julie McLaughlin, Jutta Bobbenkamp, Karen Matthews, Kathleen Maunsell-Cogley, Katie Cresswell, Kelly Love, Linda Fairbrother, Liz Fincham, Maddi Nicholson, Maggie Boyle, Maggie Welton, Malcolm Perkins, Marc Owen, Margaret Bourke, Mark Featherstone Witty, Martin Milner, Martin Pauline, Martin Perkins, Martin Wilyman, Martin Wright, Max Rubin, Melonie Anderson, Michael Nurse, Michael Walsh, Nick French, Ossie Omar, Pamela Nash, Peter Lubej, Phil Hopson, Rachael Phelps, Rea Deen-Owen, Rebecca Blackwood, Rez Kabir, Robert Coyne, Roy Apps, Roy Warren, Roz McKenzie, Ruth Basten, Ruth Pringle, Sara Brown, Sarah Llewellyn, Sarah Manton, Sally Ann Panter, Sheila Kennedy, Tayo Aluko, Teresa Cremin, Tim Hatton, Tim Pike, Tina Carroll, Tommy Mcardle, Tony Ealey, Tony Lawson, Vicki Carter, Vilde Rainbow, Vorn Cruickshank and Werner Steinhauser.

A very special thanks to Mike Gibson and Mark Bond Webster for close reading and essential editing recommendations.

SCORE CARDS

Warm Up: One day I will play Roger Federer at Wimbledon and beat Him.

First Set: How to Play Tennis.
How to deal with the irritation of 13-year olds on the other side of the net (0-1)
How to enjoy net play (0-2)
How to fly solo in a doubles pair (1-2)
How to play percentage tennis (1-3)
How to cope when the wheels fall off your game (1-4)
How Hawkeye stops us from telling the real sports stories (2-4)
Rafa Nadal is better than me (in your dreams, Rafa): or, how to develop your own internal monologue (2-5)
The mysteries of the grass court and why the sun struggles to set on the British Empire (2-6)

Second Set: How to Win at Wimbledon.
I've got into the first round at Wimbledon! (1-0)
Everyone loves a success! (2-0)
Not everyone loves a success (2-1)
Not everyone loves a success, but someone loves this one (3-1)
Success is an instrument of torture (3-2)
Success is an instrument for the torture of others (4-2)
Hanging around with the guys and preparing for greatness (4-3)
Shakespeare is walking the hallowed Wimbledon turf (5-3)
Dashed dreams and future horizons (5-4)
Ukrainian magic is no match for English guile (5-5)
The draw, the superstition and Quantum Physics (6-5)
Could it be magic? (7-5)
The signs, signifiers and signatures of tennis semiotics (8-5)
Preparation is for wimps (9-5)
I sing the tennis apotheosis and recreate the Empire (10-5)
I AM Andy Murray and have beaten Roger Federer (albeit vicariously) (11-5)

Third Set: How to become Sports Personality of the Year.
Gutted. Roasted. Fuming. (0-1)

Sports Personality Of The Year? "You're 'avin' a larf." (0-2)

Sports Personality Of The Year? Moi? (1-2)

Practicing my personality for SPOTY (2-2)

What exactly is a 'sports personality?' (3-2)

How to mount a charm offensive (3-3)

How to deal with the rumour mill that is the international tennis circuit (4-3)

I'm SPOTY! No, I'm SPOTY! Why is SPOTY becoming more like Spartacus every day? (5-3)

Living the life of Reilly with Grace dispensing favours (6-3)

Fourth Set: How to Win Power, Authority and Influence.
Waiting for my man (0-1)

Speechless in Strathclyde (0-2)

Broke, battered but not yet beaten (0-3)

iAndrew Murray Ltd is not a figment of your imagination (1-3)

God bless Roger Federer and all who sail in him (2-3)

Andy – Rafa – Novi – Serena? Who you gonna call? Club Members! (3-3)

Why Rafa Nadal is not going to make it (4-3)

Why Novak Djokovich is not going to make it (5-3)

Why Serena Williams is not going to make it (6-3)

Shock horror early exit of Nadal and Williams (7-3)

Late breaking news from The Daily Record (8-3)

The Jeremy Paxman interview on Newsnight (9-3)

Thank you HRH QE2: the future of Scottish tennis has never looked brighter (10-3)

The last post before the brand-new dawn (11-3)

Notice of suspension of club member (0-6)

Fifth Set: Tie Breaker.
The All-New Liverpool Daily Post est arrivé! Strange sightings at Otterspool Prom (0-1)

The All-New Liverpool Daily Post: New Year's fires perplex local fire services in South Liverpool (0-2)

The All-New Liverpool Daily Post: mystery arsonist found hiding on allotment (0-3)

Final Score

WARM UP:
ONE DAY
I WILL
PLAY ROGER
FEDERER AT
WIMBLEDON AND
BEAT
HIM.

ONE DAY I WILL PLAY ROGER FEDERER AT WIMBLEDON AND BEAT HIM

When I was younger, I used to watch the tennis on the TV and especially the guys like McEnroe, Borg and Nastase. Round about Wimbledon time, my brother Alex and I would play a kind of tennis out on our grandfather's lawn. I would take on the role of John McEnroe and he would enact Jimmy Connors. I would invariably win as I was fourteen and he was eleven. It was all to do with our ages and nothing to do with the fact that I had a proper tennis racket, he had a wobbly piece of cardboard, I knew how to score properly, and he didn't.

All the players we watched were whatever age they were, Alex was the age he was, and I was the age I was. Back then, tennis proficiency was all about age. I thought that the pros were pros because they were just a bit older than me, but I could see a time when I would be a bit older and be able to play them at Wimbledon.

As I've gotten older, that vision hasn't faded. I still watch tennis, see these young athletes play their hearts out and still think, one day when I'm older I shall be playing them at Wimbledon and probably beating them. Trouble is, whilst I seem to have gotten older during that time, the tennis players have gotten younger. At this rate I shall be 80 and still aiming to play the young bucks who will become the Federers of their generation.

However, as I've gotten older, it's become clearer that proficiency in tennis is not all about age. It's clear that one's tennis prowess isn't what it might be and that for all the manuals, online tutorials and shouty motivational websites there is nothing available for the tennis player of a certain age that can help propel them and their game into a different league and help bring their dreams to fruition.

This book aims to address that gap.

Part one offers you a veritable cornucopia of playing tips and tricks which will help you deal with all sorts of opponents of all sorts of sizes and shapes, playing all kind of strange shots in the oddest of circumstances.

Part two shows you how to apply those skills and strategies to go on and win a major international tennis tournament. And I should know, because that's exactly what I did at Wimbledon in July 2013.

Impressed? You will be.

Part three offers excellent advice on how to deal with the media interest and the furore around becoming an international tennis superstar and Sports Personality of the Year to boot. This is not for the faint hearted.

My book though is not just for aspirant tennis players of a certain or any age: it is for everyone who has suffered at the hands of pomposity or institutional inertia and feels that the traditional English values of fair play, a stiff upper lip and self-deprecation are lacking in many areas of our public life. With this in mind, part four offers some hard-fought wisdom about how to deal with the Machiavellian politics of the sports club – and by extension our Great British society as a whole. But having said that, sat where I am these days, dear reader, Britain is not as 'Great' as it might like to think it is. But all will be revealed as you read on.

In the meantime, let us follow the tradition of tennis clubs around the world and start our adventure together with these immortal words: Play On! Love All!

FIRST SET:
HOW TO PLAY
TENNIS.

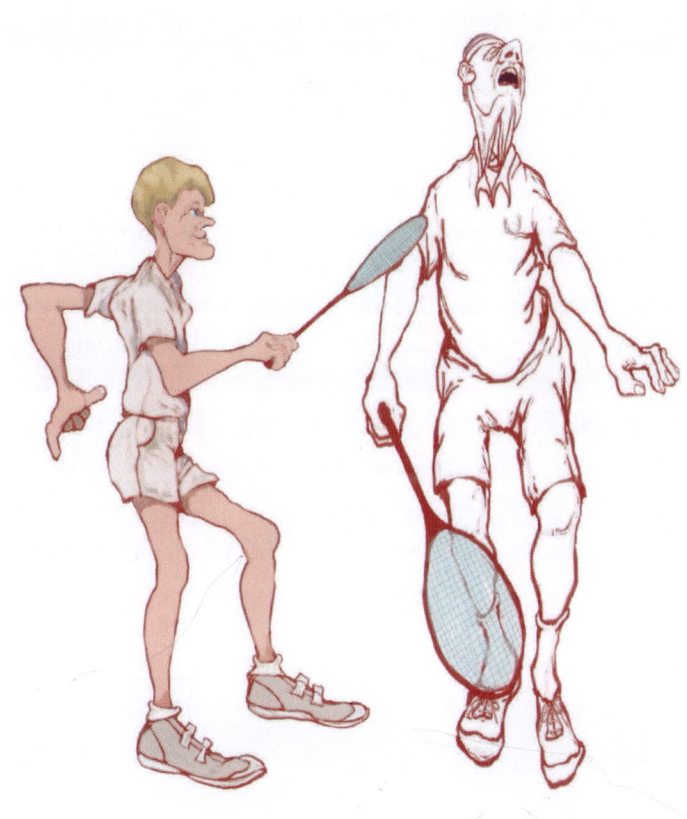

HOW TO DEAL WITH THE IRRITATION OF 13 YEAR OLDS ON THE OTHER SIDE OF THE NET (0-1)

Our team's youth policy is still in an embryonic stage (i.e. non-existent) so we increasingly find ourselves up against teams which include a couple of players whose combined ages are probably no more than twenty-two. Given our combined ages are closer to three hundred, the sight of those young lads on the other side of the net tends to fill us with some trepidation.

We view their presence initially with a degree of benign paternalism. They're learning the tennis ropes of course; learning important socialising skills (like buying a round after the match) and knowing how to respect their elders. Naturally, their learning takes different forms and sometimes you wonder if they are really learning the lessons you are trying to teach them. Sometimes, as the ball whistles past your head, for example, you wonder if they are really showing the kind of deference that is expected of them.

As the match grinds on, you increasingly become aware that deference is the last thing on their minds.

They are more intent on spinning their rackets in the air like quasi cowboys spinning their rifles. They seem to take huge delight in smashing the ball at you rather than past you and can't suppress their giggles as they manoeuvre you around the court, making you run this way and that, putting great strain on your knees and ankles, before putting you out of your misery by delicately dropping a shot just over the net when you're stood panting on the base line, wondering where all your sprinting skills have gone.

The challenge for us ageing tennis players, is to look those young bucks in the eye, suppress feelings of irritation, alarm and envy, and try to rediscover the athleticism which deserted us decades ago. Wearing our tennis caps the wrong way around a la Leyton Hewitt is not the answer.

HOW TO ENJOY NET PLAY (0-2)

"Go stand at the net," your partner says to you one evening. *"I'll take the base line."*

The chance to stand at the net and effect impressive volleys which win points, seal games and lead to early evening glory is always a cheerful moment in the career of the ageing tennis player. It allows you to recapture the gazelle like bounce in your step, to tap into hidden reserves of aggression and alpha male behaviour and rekindle past ambitions of beating Nastase at his own game.

The trouble is, playing at the net these days is more a case of fending off the ennui – not to mention despair - rather than infuriating your opponent with deft sharp shots at impossibly cute angles.

You take up your position at the net, crouching, on the balls of your feet, ready for the moment. Your partner serves; the return is cross court back to her. She returns the return, cross court. You stand and stare, ready for the moment. The returned return is returned, again cross court, just out of your reach. Better not go for that you tell yourself and continue your standing and staring but wondering when the moment is going to come. The cross-court dialogue continues. You and your opposite partner are like guests in the lounge at student parties looking at all the couples coupling up late at night on the floor, on the sofas, on the staircase. All you can do is stand and stare and wonder and look at your watch and start to get bored.

When suddenly there's a change of action.

The ball is heading towards you at a medium pace. You see it. It's as huge as a football, the court is wide open, you're going to smash it to the left, no, hang on, you're going to drop it to the right, no no no you're going to volley it down the line…. You step forward with three different plans in your head ready to bathe in the glory of the decisive winner, but you hit the damn thing so hard off the racket handle the ball sails up and over your own head, backwards. The point is lost, your moment is gone, and your partner is looking at you in exasperation.

"Sorry partner," you offer cheerily; but deep down that lost opportunity will eat away at you all night and you will hang your head in shame until the bar kicks you out at way past midnight.

Life at the net offers you so much potential glory – and equally large amounts of regret for lost opportunities and missed moments.

HOW TO FLY SOLO IN A DOUBLES PAIR (1-2)

One of the mirages about doubles tennis is that you and a partner play against two other people who also call themselves partners. The core idea of the game is that it's two against two, each partner of the pair taking on a different role in their team, complementing the other's skills and working in tune with each other and the ebb and flow of the game. So far, so perfect.

Unfortunately, the complexity of the league that is the North West Division section 5(d) means that the partner you play with varies from week to week. One night you'll be coupled with the lean and fit Czech coach, Ivan, who is recovering from tennis elbow, the next you'll be playing with the equivalent of Shrek. It's also not lost on you that your new partner is staring at you at the start of the evening with a look that varies from admiration to disgust – often over the course over the first point of the first game.

As the game progresses your attention turns from how you're going to get the ball back over the net to what on earth that idiot is doing behind you. Why is the ball taking so long to reach the other side? Why has she stopped running from side to side as you try to mount an attack at the front of the court, guarding the net from any enemy incursions? Why on earth is she making that revolting Sharipova-style shrieking?

Before long the grim truth is out. You are no longer playing two against two: it's you against three and the third opponent is on the same side of the net as you.

Playing doubles is a fine aspiration but when you realise that your so-called partner has inadvertently turned into your opponent, it's time to take the game into your own hands. You must go down all guns blazing. You probably won't win the match, and you'll certainly make an enemy for life, but at least you can say you survived the treachery that is the imperfect doubles game.

HOW TO PLAY PERCENTAGE TENNIS (1–3)

Many of us in the tennis elite that is the North West Division section 5(d) frequently find ourselves with a stark choice at key moments in any game. Do we go for glory and smash the living smithereens out of the tennis ball that is fast approaching us and everything that then stands in the way of our killer return? Or do we pragmatically and tentatively hope for just one thing: to get the ball back over the net, preferably within the off-putting white lines that are referred to, in the tennis trade, as the line markings (base lines, service lines, side lines and the like).

This is technically referred to as playing percentage tennis and alludes to a mind-set which requires the more ambitious players to consider the likelihood of pulling off that backhand overhead volley (with added top spin for good measure) deep into the opponent's court – or whether the greater risk is that the ball will just fall feebly at their feet.

Percentage tennis – and its attendant cousin, risk aversion – are not the best friends of the ageing tennis player. For us, playing percentages is the kind of attitude that summarises all that is wrong with the state of British Tennis.

Playing percentages is for the feeble and the fearsome.

It is witnessed daily in the offices of the tennis club and other amateur establishments who spurn the opportunity to lead their sport into the brave new world of world domination. It is the kind of tennis which won no fair hearts, no fair maidens or even half decent trophies.

Are John McEnroe or Serena Williams famed for their caution or risk aversion? Do we stand in awe of Roger Federer or Martina Navratilova because they have completed a risk awareness analysis with particular skill? Do Novak Djokovic and Rafa Nadal ever fill in a health and safety form before they face each other in one of their regular matches-of-the-century?

Of course not.

Neither should ageing tennis players. Our careers are dependent on much more important things than having to worry about whether the ball was in or out, whether it got over the net, or whether we hit the ball at all.

The health of the tennis elite that is the North West Division section 5(d) is in our fearless hands and all the better for it.

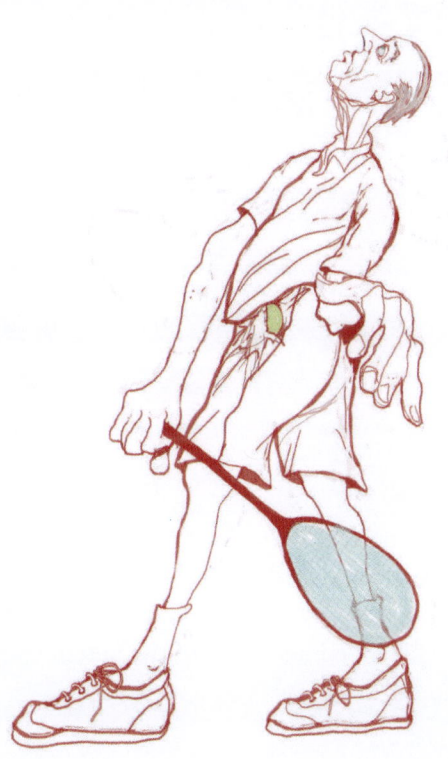

HOW TO COPE WHEN THE WHEELS FALL OFF YOUR GAME (1–4)

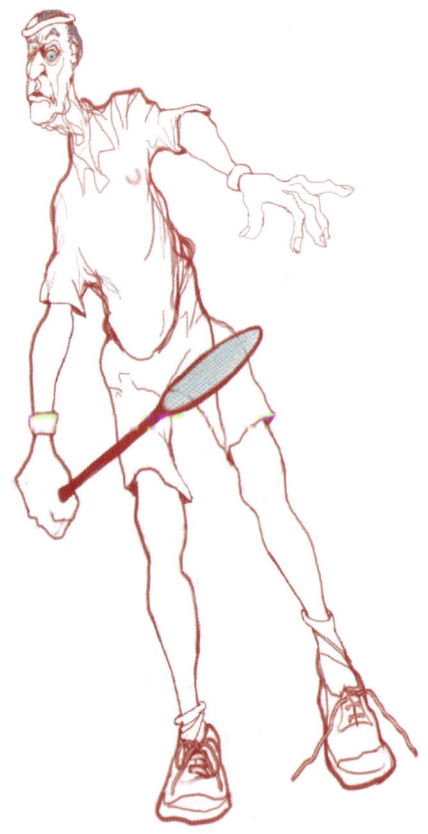

There's no getting away from the sad truth that however much coaching you buy from your friendly neighbourhood tennis coach – Ivan, a big Czech bruiser with calf muscles the size of your waistline and who serves at you with the ferocity of a cruise missile - there will come a time in the match when the wheels fall off your game completely.

Whether this be your serve (last week so reliable, this week so pathetic), your volley (last week so punishing, this week so useless) or your eyesight (last night so keen, this morning so bleary), there is no getting away from the fact that for some mysterious reason your body has decided that enough is enough and it refuses to do what you need it to do, when you need to do it. You may as well book an appointment with your knees a week in advance to make sure they bend when you want them to.

When this happens, there are various options. Turn on yourself with complete and utter self-loathing, tell yourself what a pathetic specimen of humankind you really are, and punish yourself not only throughout the game but for the rest of the afternoon. Turn on your racket, mutilate it and throw it to the nearest pack of savage hounds. Or turn on your opponents and accuse them of cheating at every possible opportunity.

This is much the best strategy.

Yell at them loudly, pointing out that they're calling the line wrong; they're foot faulting; they're serving into the light. You will soon unsettle them enough for the wheels to come off their game leaving them to flounder around like hysterical porpoises on the courts whilst the rest of the world looks on in complete disinterest.

You may never successfully re-attach the wheels to your game again that afternoon, but at least you will have entertained the passing geese as they fly overhead, attracted by your screaming and self-immolation.

HOW HAWKEYE STOPS US FROM TELLING THE REAL SPORTS STORIES (2–4)

Our club has recently invested in Hawkeye; not the hi-tech line calling assessment tool so beloved of fans at Wimbledon, but several casks of a local brewery's best foaming draught bitter.

It's a fraction of the cost of its technological namesake (only £2.45 a pint) but the effect is much the same. Three pints of the stuff (7.7% ABV) downed in quick succession give the recipient extraordinary visual acuity; so much so that they can see whether a ball is in, out or shaken all about - along with Mother Hokey Cokey -from a distance of three tennis courts away.

Our Hawkeye has the additional benefit of giving its recipient forceful and vocal opinions to support its unquestionable line call judgements.

But our Hawkeye suffers from the same defect that its technological cousin has. The unerring sense that it is right, 100% of the time, come rain, sun, wind or hail. Hawkeye Bitter doesn't allow for any interpretation or split second of momentary doubt about whether a ball was in or out. It either IS or it ISN'T.

This dehumanises the game of tennis in the same way that goal line technology is dehumanising football and means that these most strenuous of human endeavours will no longer be encapsulated in myths and stories which prop up the game as much as the millions of dollars which prop up the games' administrators.

Those myths – Geoff Hurst's 'goal' against Germany, Maradona's 'Hand of God', the plainly wrong Hawkeye call that judged my shot out at the end of the super tie-break on Sunday (a call which meant we lost the game, set, match and evening) – are what keep us playing and watching, irrespective of the accuracy of the judgement.

Hawkeye may well be watching the game more closely than humans can – but if we're not careful, we'll stop watching altogether, bored with the predictability and infallibility of the bitter drinker and his hi-tech observational equivalent.

RAFA NADAL IS BETTER THAN ME (IN YOUR DREAMS, RAFA): OR, HOW TO DEVELOP YOUR OWN INTERNAL MONOLOGUE (2-5)

As I convincingly hit my fourth double fault of the game into the net, my tennis partner astutely noticed that I was not as good a tennis player as Rafa Nadal. This was a bit of a shock as I had been modelling myself on Rafa all afternoon - a grunt here, a sneer there, and a regal Hispanic wave as I cruised to a 6-0 6-0 6-0 victory in front of the club house and its assembled crowd of committee members, fellow players and astonished 13 year olds.

"Not only can I be like Rafa, I am Rafa!" my internal monologue told me, as I continued to invent all the available scenarios at full pelt. This was just before the wheels came off my serve and I lost the game in a blaze of ignominy.

That's the trouble with internal monologues. They carry you away to golden lands of opportunity, trophies and a jet setting lifestyle of tennis clubs in the Algarve, private yachts and afternoon tea on the centre of Centre Court before you've even remembered who won the toss to start the game.

What they don't do is allow you to be in the moment, to focus on the here and now. They insist you dwell on the there and then, and at the very least have you back in the clubhouse signing autographs before you've hit the first serve of the afternoon.

I had to concede graciously at that point. On the basis of the available evidence, I was probably not as good, that afternoon on that day, as Rafa.

But every dog has his day.

Rafa is not invincible and even an ageing tennis player might still be able to summon up an historic victory in the unlikeliest of circumstances. When you're ready, Rafa, I'm waiting for you on grass court number five. Just beware of the moving snooker balls under its surface.

THE MYSTERIES OF THE GRASS COURT AND WHY THE SUN STRUGGLES TO SET ON THE BRITISH EMPIRE (2–6)

"I don't like your attitude!" snapped the club captain to me one night as we squared up to each other over the debatable state of the club's grass courts.

"And I don't like yours!" I volleyed back at her before she swanned imperiously back off to the club house, no doubt to complete some kind of complaint form about stroppy club members who don't know a good court when they play on one.

The reason for this tiff between these members has been the cause of many more members' anguish – not to say damaged knee ligaments – in recent years.

The club's grass courts although serene to look at from over half a mile away, are actually treacherous minefields when you actually play on them. They are potholed; some have moles residing under the service lines, and, as I suggested earlier, court five has its own species of hazard under its surface - continuously moving snooker balls which shift during a point so that on one occasion a ball can bounce perfectly logically and the next it will either stop dead in its tracks; not bounce at all and roll along the ground; or rear up at you at double the pace you thought it was travelling at and strike you on the temple with all the force of a supercharged cricket ball.

The undulating surface that is court 5 has led to many a concussed ageing tennis player. Like the British Empire, you never know what you're going to get, what it'll do when it gets there and what damage it will wreak later on.

This is a problem, however, that will not only not go away, it is one that is unfixable. The grass tennis court is a source of national identity and pride that is lodged so strongly in the English psyche that no amount of damaged knees, black eyes or litigation claims will ever persuade the club committee to bite the bullet and say "Yes, grass has had its time, but no more of this antiquated surface. The way forward is Astroturf! And god bless all who play on her."

Our devotion to grass is admirable in the way it conjures up memories of Pimms, cucumber sandwiches, and serfs who know their place and maintain the right attitude to those in authority.

Nevertheless, in the 21st century, these memories of empire enshrined on our grass courts continue to cause lasting damage not just to the political terrain, but, more importantly, to our knees as well.

It's about time we concreted over the lot of them. The courts that is, not our knees.

SECOND SET:
HOW TO WIN
AT WIMBLEDON.
(FIRST SET: 2–6)

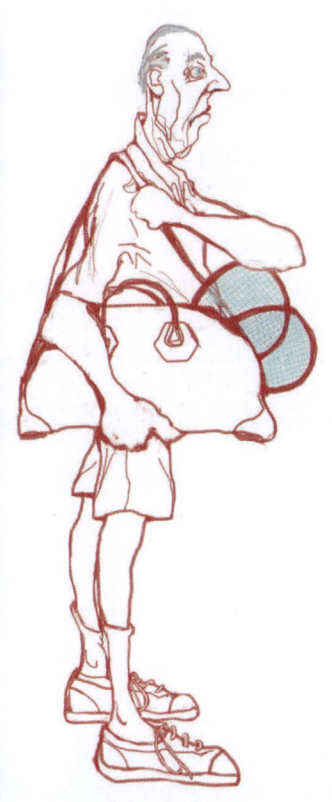

I'VE GOT INTO THE FIRST ROUND AT WIMBLEDON! (1-0)

I never thought I'd see the day but my wild-card entry at Wimbledon finally came through yesterday. Apparently, there'd been a mix up between the LTA and the local clubs in the North West Division section 5(d) that caused several players who had been awarded wild cards to not be informed of their fortune and so they didn't turn up. Their fortune-turned-misfortune turned into my fortune when I got the call from the guys in the blazers at Wimbledon - probably the best tennis club in the world (notwithstanding the Carling claim of supreme ownership). I had to get onto court 32 at 7.30 in order to complete my first, first-round match against the Serbian thirteen-year-old, Slobodan Slobovitch.

Imagine! Me at Wimbledon!

After so many years spent enviously watching all those bright young things slugging it out on the green and pleasant lawns of Jerusalem!

The best was yet to come. I turned up on time to find the 13-year-old loitering on court, clearly nervous at the prospect of playing a more seasoned campaigner. And he had every right to be nervous. Before long I was in the zone. The ball was as big as a football in my eyes and flying at the pace of a snail. I picked off every shot with ease. I played my best high risk, low percentage tennis ever. I was living in the moment. I was in the here and the now. I felt immortal.

It was all over before I realised it and I had beaten him 6-0, 6-0, 7-6 with the tie-break going to a massive 26-24 point game.

He was devastated. Afterwards, he slumped, a broken figure, on the side of the court. His father couldn't console him, but both had the good grace to shake hands with me before we left the court at shortly after 9pm.

So, I am through to the second round, and due to play early tomorrow afternoon. It has been an amazing adventure so far and anything in future is a bonus.

EVERYONE LOVES A SUCCESS! (2-0)

I'm amazed how popular I've become on the tennis circuit ever since getting through to the second round at Wimbledon. I'm getting phone calls asking me whether I'd like to join a doubles team with the German, Gerd Fistingburger (no. 944 in the world) and a mixed doubles pair with the British woman from Acton, Julia Spetsi – our one-time no. 64.

I've declined all their offers as I want to focus on my singles journey. But this recognition by other players in the tennis fraternity is both gratifying and humbling - success breeds interest and everyone wants to get a bit of the action, in whatever way they can. Indeed, I've even alarmed myself by thinking about 'going pro' as the guys in the locker room call it. Still, I manage to rein in my ambitions and ground myself in the realities of the here and now.

I'll need to keep my eyes on the skyline, feet on the Astroturf and get a new racket as well. That wooden one is well past its prime.

NOT EVERYONE LOVES
A SUCCESS (2-1)

I was shocked earlier tonight when I was hanging around the locker room (as the guys calls it) to find that, contrary to my belief that everyone (i.e. the guys) would be pleased for me and my early wild-card success, that there are certain tennis players (so-called professionals) who are actually quite dismissive of my achievement so far.

I heard one of them muttering rudely about the wild-card system and using words like '*loser*' and '*amateur*' and '*tosser*' in the same sentence. When I tried confronting him with a hard stare, he just stared back, spat out his chewing gum at me, and fiercely pulled on his tennis hat backwards, in that irritating Leyton Hewitt style. And no, it wasn't LH - he's much too much a sporting gentleman to drop his standards so far.

No, I think it was a mate of the person who was my prospective doubles partner, Gerd Fistingburger, a Frenchman called Alois. He may have taken offence at my earlier jokey attempt to engage him in some 'Allo 'Allo banter *('allo 'allo Alois, how's life in Rheinland Pfalz?*) but I can't be too sure. I'm pretty sure though I saw the two of them in the showers whispering to each other and casting me baleful glances in between washing each other down.

But his hostility has certainly been a wake-up call and has shown me another side to the green and pleasant lawns of Jerusalem.

I'll have to tread carefully tomorrow in my second-round match – which, incidentally, I've just found out, is against the Croatian, Milos Milosovich, a very handy player I'm told, who specialises in long baseline rallies but is terrified to get too close to the net. I'll need to get some more practice in tonight. I'll just finish this pint and get on court with the guys until the sun goes down. Wish me well!

But if you're Alois – you can go stick your racket up your arschloch.

NOT EVERYONE LOVES A SUCCESS, BUT SOMEONE LOVES THIS ONE (3-1)

I now have a coach. As I was finishing my preparations last night for what is undoubtedly the biggest game of my life – a 2nd round match against the Croat, Milos Milosovich, out on Court 28 sometime this afternoon if you've not been paying attention (do please keep up), a middle age woman approached me wearing a rain coat with a sack load of tennis rackets slung over her shoulder. Her trainers had seen better days and suggested she wouldn't be prancing around on a tennis court any time soon.

She looked at me somewhat askance and asked a couple of searching questions about my game; questions about things like my stance, my grip and what lager I'd been drinking earlier. I replied – out of curiosity more than anything else – and the next thing she offers me is her coaching services on a no win, no fee basis.

This struck me as too good an offer to turn down, so I signed on the dotted line there and then. Mrs Hacienda Buscando Stanley Carter (I'm allowed to call her Hac for short) is now my official coach for the remainder of Wimbledon – and who knows what will happen after that.

Look out Milos Milosovich!

I'm armed and dangerous and loaded with advice and guidance from one of Wimbledon's surprise results: the coach and mentor that is Mrs Hacienda Buscando Stanley Carter (or Hac, for short).

And it's certainly been a 'Winning-bledon so far this week - boom boom!

SUCCESS IS AN INSTRUMENT OF TORTURE (3–2)

I'm fuming. Absolutely fuming.

I've just come off court after what must have been one of the most ridiculous days in recent Wimbledon history. And it's all down to the prancing and preening of several so-called tennis VIPs and pros and their ilk.

When the chalk dust settles, I shall have strong words with the blazers, leather arm patches, twinsets and pearls that make up the LTA establishment, make no mistake.

The morning had started so well. I started my match against Milos Milosovich (Croatian, court 28, 2nd round if you've not kept up) in reasonable form. Not great, I grant you, but certainly reasonable. I was 0-5 down after eight minutes and he was playing like a possessed Balkan demon, but I was holding my nerve, if nothing else.

But then lo and bloody behold who appears court side as I serve to save the first set? None other than the sneering Gerd Fistingburger and his mate Alois, both wearing ridiculously expensive wrap around shades and their baseball caps shoved firmly the wrong way around on their short-cropped heads.

I catch them out of the corner of my eye as I bounce the ball eight times prior to my specialist underarm serve and one of them yells 'fault' at the top of his tinny little continental voice and I promptly belt the ball right up and out over the court towards Henman Hill.

I duly protest straight after this outlandish behaviour but am cautioned by the so-called umpire. Five seconds later he's given me another caution for racket abuse.

Now, I will admit my racket is no great technological marvel – but it's well versed in being kicked around tennis courts and is used to a volley of expletives if it gives up on me at crucial times. It's used to a bit of abuse – it's why we get on so well and it's the main reason I've got this far in my tennis career (such as it is).

So, giving me a caution for treating my racket with the contempt it occasionally deserves is like the proverbial suspect line call to a McEnroe. Needless to say, I lose the first set 0-6 and a red mist descends all around me as I struggle to compete in the second. I look around for my coach, Hac, but she's nowhere to be seen.

It goes from bad-to-worse. Not only do Gerd and Alois put their feet up on the railings and snigger and giggle at my hapless progress, but they're joined by the other player whose advances I spurned, Julia Spetsi – so called due to her tendency to mix Coca Cola and Fanta in between sets.

She adds to my general misery by outrageously flirting with one of the line judges at crucial times. Eight times my serve goes in, eight times he calls it out after she has distracted him with her fluttering eyelashes. Before I know it I am 0-3 down in the second and the world is imploding.

Slowly though. It implodes very, very slowly. The ball slows right down. I run at the pace of a slug. The crowd applauds as if it's in a trance. The seagulls over-head seem to hover for ever, and you can see their droppings leaving their backsides and falling slowly, inevitably and inexorably towards the umpire's head. I think about warning him but it's pointless. The way this tennis universe is operating, my warning would take over a week to reach his ears.

Before I know it, I've lost the second set 0-6 and I'm in the process of repeating the experience in the third set.

I get to 0-5 down and have to serve to save the match when all of sudden Hac appears at the side of the court and the heavens open.

The rain comes down unlike any other day in Wimbledon history and the umpire has no choice but to postpone proceedings and get the BBG onto the court, dragging the covers behind them.

I look at Milos and shrug my shoulders. There's not a lot I can do about the English weather. I apologise but he ignores me, packs his bags and scarpers off to the locker room.

Meanwhile, Hac brusquely takes my racket off me, swops it for another black and gold version, and tells me to go practice against a wall until it stops raining.

At two sets down and 0-5 down in the third, I really can't see the point of it now. My so-called success at Wimbledon has become an instrument of torture.

But I do as she suggests, penning letters of complaint in my mind to keep the boredom of hitting balls against a wall at bay. We're back on court later this afternoon to no doubt finish off what has been an excruciating morning.

The sooner I can get the hell out of Kansas the better.

SUCCESS IS AN INSTRUMENT FOR THE TORTURE OF OTHERS (4-2)

This 'Black Wednesday' of Wimbledon is delivering more than its fair share of thrills, spills and unfortunate injuries today.

From the unenviable position of being two sets down, 0-5 down in the third, and facing almost guaranteed elimination within two minutes of returning to court after rain stopped play, I am amazed – sobered even – to report that the 'Black Wednesday' curse of unexpected injury has affected my match too.

My opponent – the Croatian, Milos Milosovich – returned to the locker room in the break during our game. He cooled down; he rested; he kept warm; he had a light lunch - and as they were announcing our return to court he immediately came down with a terrible bout of gastroenteritis (so the guys in the locker room are saying).

He was doubled up with pain and had to retire from the match with immediate effect. I felt quite sorry for him as things were going so well, from his point of view at least.

Not that sorry, mind you. His departure means that I am through to the third round.

I am of course over the moon despite Milos being as sick as a parrot. I accept that this is possibly one of the unlikeliest outcomes ever in the circumstances but tennis, as my newfound coach, Hac, reminded me, is a funny old game. You never know when a knee injury or gastroenteritis are going to strike these days, especially on grass.

So, I am now preparing for my next opponent - the Bosnian, Djelko Djelkovich, a player I've never heard of before.

But that doesn't matter.

I'm into the third round at Wimbledon and anything is possible.

HANGING AROUND WITH THE GUYS AND PREPARING FOR GREATNESS (4-3)

One of the benefits of qualifying for the third round at Wimbledon is that you eventually get to hang out with the guys – not only in the locker room but also out in civvy street - as they call it. Check this out: Stan (Wrawinka), Rafa (Nadal), Andy (Murray) and myself all went to the Pizza Hut up Tooting High Street tonight so that we could compare how our respective tournaments were going.

Stan (W) was a bit miffed at his first round exit as was Rafa (N) of course – in fact, he was inconsolable until we plied him with flaming Sambucas, and he loosened up. Andy (M) and I discussed the finer points of the overhead backhand volley and he asked for my opinion about the current fashion for wearing your socks down around your ankles. I told him he shouldn't preoccupy himself with such trivial things, but I detect a sense of anxiety from Andy (M) every time someone mentions his socks.

I decided this might affect be affecting his mental preparation for future games and made a mental note to draw attention to them, should we find ourselves battling it out for a place in the final.

Or even – perish the thought - Battling for 'The Final' itself.

I daren't look at the draw in case it tempts fate but a final with Andy (M) would certainly look good at my home club and would teach those committee members a thing or two about how to dress.

Plus, of course, the press would love an all-British final. Something I don't think has ever happened in Wimbledon history – or for that matter, any Grand Slam tournament in the world, ever.

So, the weight of history hangs heavy on the shoulders of both me and Andy (M) and we shall have to tread carefully over the next ten days so that we brace ourselves for the media onslaught that would inevitably come our way, should we find ourselves in the Wimbledon Final.

SHAKESPEARE IS WALKING THE HALLOWED WIMBLEDON TURF (5-3)

'Black Wednesday', 'Wild Wednesday', 'Wacky Wednesday', 'Wednesday Wipe-out' - whatever you call it, our Wimbledon Wednesday had all the elements of the best of Shakespeare.

Both tragedy and comedy were never far away yesterday as player after player succumbed to the dangers of the turf.

I myself had a fortunate escape due to a combination of physical and biological elements: a storm reminiscent of *The Tempest* and a gastric bug bringing about another type of tempest deep in the bowels of my unfortunate opponent Milos Milosovich.

Not only was I victorious in the most unlikely of circumstances, I also felt vindicated in my views on the perils of playing on grass (*nota bene*, woman chairman of club tennis section, *nota bene*), so I approach today with a clear sense of destiny and purpose.

Shakespeare is clearly walking the hallowed turf of Wimbledon this week, hanging out in the locker room with the guys and I suspect he will have a ringside seat at my match with the Bosnian, Djelko Djelkovich, later today.

To coin a phrase of the famous 1960s Supermarionation show, Stingray, *'Anything can happen in the next half hour – and probably will.'*

Djelko, Novak (D) and Andy (M): you have been warned.

DASHED DREAMS AND FUTURE HORIZONS (5-4)

I was dismayed last night to find out after I'd been hanging out with Andy (M) and Rafa (N) that Roger (F) had fallen at the second hurdle of the prestigious event that is the Wimbledon Tennis Tournament.

As one who had earlier that afternoon successfully progressed to the third round, I felt for Roger and his dashed dreams. My immediate reaction was that I jump on a bus and get straight down to his penthouse suite in Putney and console him. Rafa (N) advised me against it though. He had tried such an approach a couple of years ago only for Roger (F) to set his American Pit Bull Terriers loose on him the moment he rang the doorbell.

It is difficult for someone so old to fail at such an early stage in this international competition – and to fail so badly, truth be told – but I am sure he will take it on his substantial Swiss chin and recover in the fullness of time. I sent him a text message to tell him as much and urged him not to give up.

"Think positive!" I texted him – *"but don't give up the day job either"*, I joshed with a funny little emoticon at the end of my one-hundred-and-sixty-character message. He hasn't replied yet, but I expect he's going through some tough soul searching at the moment, up there in his penthouse suite in Putney. No doubt his yappy dogs are keeping him company.

That's the trouble with being so old on the tennis circuit these days and trying to live off your past glories. You go into a game with your head in entirely the wrong place. You think you're it. You think you're invincible. You think the world owes you a living. You think you're God's gift to tennis. Just because you've got a nice penthouse suite in Putney and a family of yapping American Pitt bull terriers.

But the fact is, you're over the hill, you're long gone Daddy-oh, and there ain't no turnin' back the hands of time 'cos you gotta make way for a new generation of up and coming stars – all us tennis players who've been waiting in the wings for years and who may not have the penthouse suite in Putney, or the barking mad American Pit Bulls, but by God we have English spirit and English blood and are on the path to reclaim the 'King Of All Tennis Tournament Trophies': the Wimbledon Gentlemen's Singles Trophy.

So, when Roger (F) surfaces from his black dog depression and is ready to talk to me, I shall benignly place my hand on his shoulder, steer him gently in the direction of YouTube videos on how to play tennis and offer him a couple of ring side seats at my next match - which by the way, is my third-round tie tomorrow.

At Wimbledon.

The place where he just got eliminated from.

It may just get him in the right state of mind for his next Grand Slam tournament.

UKRAINIAN MAGIC IS NO MATCH FOR ENGLISH GUILE (5–5)

I have to admit to some unease about Roger (F)'s result and my unseemly response on his doorstep yesterday.

He didn't need to hear that from me, and I should have been back in the laager (as the guys call SW19) hitting my balls against the wall instead of berating his dogs and declining career.

But I wasn't and I wasn't. Instead, I paced around the outside courts, trying to comprehend what happened during that fateful 'Wimble-weird' Wednesday.

I became wracked with guilt as the super-moon assumed ghost like proportions and memories of my early days on the club's mini courts surrounded by traffic cones and bean bags overwhelmed me. I felt possessed. A tennis legend in his own lunch time but out of his depth. Owls flew out of the nearby poplar trees. I saw skulls of dead tennis players turn to look at me accusingly as I stalked the pathways around Court 2.

Before I know it, I'm faced with an awesome sight: not the expected lanky Bosnian, Djelko Djelkovich pacing around the court, but the Ukrainian, Sergiy Stakhovsky who just the day before was responsible for Roger (F)'s premature ejaculation from the tournament.

How could this be possible? Matches at Wimbledon couldn't just disappear, could they? It was all beginning to feel like a crazy dream.

If Sergiy was hoping to keep a low profile after his jaw-dropping victory over Roger, you certainly wouldn't know it. He had draped a huge banner over the railings which featured a Ukrainian flag and the message: "WELL DONE SERGIY – THE MAGIC WORKED".

So that's what's going on I said to myself as we warmed up. The Ukrainian summoned up the spirits of Kiev and this is what had done for Roger (F). This fellow from the Urals and his magic potions was now loudly proclaiming to a nearby camera crew:

"The night before I played Roger, the kids left a pot of chocolate spread in front of the door to our room with a sticker on it saying, 'magic recipe for Sergiy'. I had a little bit of it in the morning, so the kids were happy, and it worked. That's why I said it was magic and now I'm taking it every day because they believe in it."

I was determined that whilst he might have dispatched one of the (alleged) tennis giants of all time and fiddled with the fixtures to boot, there was no way that his hocus pocus was going to derail my ambition. I promptly set about dismantling Stakhovsky's service and all-round game. Before too long I had won the match 3 sets to 1 (6-2, 2-6, 7-5, 6-3) and Sergiy was dispatched back East with his magic potions slung over his back and his tennis racket wrapped around a lamp post in a nearby cul-de-sac - a sobering reminder of the rapid rise and even quicker fall of one of the giant killers of our tennis times.

I was on my way to the fourth round: not knowing who was next on my list but determined to make up for my part in avenging Roger (F)'s downfall. Ukrainian chocolate magic my arse.

THE DRAW, THE SUPERSTITION AND QUANTUM PHYSICS (6–5)

The phone has been ringing constantly on this supposedly quiet Wimbledon Sunday. Many club members (woman chairman excepted – surprise, surprise), have been offering their support in the unlikeliest of ways. Some have offered to carry my racket; others have offered to stitch their logo into my t-shirt. One wise crack offered me a day's intensive training.

Me and training! Imagine that!

But they're all asking the same question: What do you rate your chances in the 4th round?

And they then proceed to tell me the potential matches I could be facing should I, by the wildest stretch of their imaginations, be successful tomorrow when play resumes.

They talk in hushed tones of finals with either Andy or Noli. They summon up huge successful lottery applications for the club itself. They imagine fending off the press on a daily basis. They even rashly devise plans to improve our own grass courts. It's at this point I know we have entered a quantum universe where nothing is what it appears to be.

I then tell them in no uncertain terms that every player has their own superstitions to get through a tournament and mine is a simple one - don't look at the draw, don't plan to play anyone in particular, but just turn up on court at the right time and see who turns up. The habit I have developed is based on Heisenberg's uncertainty principle - the more I know, the less likely I am likely to win. Conversely, the more ignorant I remain, the greater the likelihood of my success.

This strikes many of the committee as being a bit foolhardy but in comparison with other Wimbledon superstitions – shoelace colours, number of steps from court side chair to the baseline, jumping up and down in front of your opponent when the umpire's tossing his coin – not knowing the draw is as logical as any of them.

And let's face it, if any tennis player believes their little acts of superstition and habit can influence a result for the positive, then my superstition is no better or worse than theirs. One thing it does prove - the tennis universe is no longer Newtonian. We're into parallel universes, relativity theory and time-space continuum warps complete with Einstein-Rosen bridges, Black Holes and String Theory to boot. It's no accident that quantum theory describes so accurately what it's like to play on grass.

Not knowing the draw allows for the random and the unexpected, and one thing I do know, is that I'm going to need plenty of quark, strangeness and charm to progress through the remaining rounds at Wimbledon this year.

So to all you committee members and followers out there: please keep me in the dark about the supposed logic of the draw and allow for a little bit of relativity theory to make its mark on proceedings this week.

COULD IT BE MAGIC?
(7–5)

Sue Barker called it Magic Monday and I have to say she's not wrong.

As far as I'm concerned, as long as its followed up with a thaumaturgic Tuesday, another weird Wednesday, an unearthly Thursday and a freakish Friday, then I don't mind as my chances of appearing in the final are inexplicably shortening day by wondrous day.

So, is this what they mean by the enchantment of Wimbledon?

Tennis players young and old, amateur and professional, skilled or incompetent alike all in thrall to the superstitions, the voodoo and the hiatus that the tournament brings around every year.

I am, as the 13-year olds in our neck of the woods say, living it large.

Not least because I have just trounced Serena Williams, the lady's number one seed over 3 scintillating sets. She was aghast, I was astonished, Sue Barker for once was speechless.

Magic Monday indeed!

Watch out Andy and Noli: nothing can stop me now. See you both in the final!

THE SIGNS, SIGNIFIERS AND SIGNATURES OF TENNIS SEMIOTICS (8-5)

The tension's mounting as we head towards the last three days of the epic tournament that is the Wimbledon Championships of the All England Club.

The signs of my potential progress through the next rounds are encouraging and I feel I am finally being treated with the respect that is due a wild card who has achieved more than anyone's wildest imaginings could have foreseen.

The groundsmen tug their collective forelocks as I pass them by. The guys in the locker room go silent when I enter (a sure sign of respectful awe). And even my one-time adversaries, Gerd Fistingburger and Alois, have taken to stepping aside when I approach them, their heads bowed, eyes averted (both gestures, significant signifiers of shame).

I sense a victory of massive proportions on the horizon.

Even Mrs Lady Chairman, to my great surprise, phoned this morning ostensibly to ask how the courts were behaving themselves, although I knew this meant that she was dying to ingratiate herself with me. I was able to point her, without the slightest hint of sarcasm, to the list of casualties those accursed surfaces have been responsible for over the first week of the competition. She didn't listen, as per, and even had the effrontery to ask if I could get Andy (M) to sign her grandson's tennis shorts for her. I assured her that my signature would cost a lot less. But she was having none of that either, made some rude remark about my attitude (again) and swanned off the phone (again) no doubt to start constructing a well-executed complaint (again).

So whilst there are many pointers to my impending resurrection in my local club, there is still a job to be done at the top of the political pile. My mission will not be complete until I have the trophy in hand, the cheque in the bank and Mrs Lady Chairman waving the white flag of surrender.

PREPARATION IS FOR WIMPS (9–5)

Well, whether I like it or not, I now know my opponent for the final match of this year's Wimbledon men's tennis finals. I have tried in my silly, superstitious way to avoid looking at the draw, but after yesterday there can be no avoiding the truth of who is left in the championship.

So, it'll be him and me again. We've had some epic ventures in our time, and this looks like being yet another one.

So, how to prepare?

Hac, my coach suggests saunas, gluten free pasta and a spot of practice on the Virtua Tennis 4 Xbox console. I'm more inclined to hit a few balls at the BBGs who line up at the back of the practice courts at this time of year, puffing on a few illicit ciggies before they're called to bow and curtsey to the great and the good. Avoiding my power packed service will definitely keep them on their toes.

On the other hand, it's now too late to prepare for anything other than what the final result will be. There's a lot spoken in elite sporting circles (the ones I frequent) about failing to prepare and preparing to fail: but my view is that preparation is a much over-rated pastime and that we would all be a lot better off if we lived in the heat of the moment, in the hustle and bustle of the here and now, rather than worry in advance about this particular shot, or that particular action.

Tennis is a sport – take it from me – which requires its players to get in the zone, stay there and don't leave it until the last BBG has picked up your drenched towel off the grass and you have shaken hands with HRH and banked the cheque.

And that means hoofing it down to the pub for a couple of last-minute pints of our landlord's best foaming Hawkeye Bitter before casually sauntering down to Centre Court some time tomorrow, ready to take my place in history.

I SING THE TENNIS APOTHEOSIS
AND RECREATE THE EMPIRE (10–5)

I walk through my apartment door in SW19 and I'm bowled over.

Not in a cricketing sense you understand, but by the public response to my impending Wimbledon final tomorrow afternoon.

There are bouquets of flowers from admirers all over the world - from Serbia and Scotland, from the USofA to the Straits of Menai via the bars of Dublin - which reach from the floor to the ceiling. There are cards, and more cards, telegrams and yet more cards. So many cards and begging letters that I lose count. There are faxes and reams of emails and final demands by the shed load. I gather them all up and drop them in the bath. I can look at them later.

There are sponsors' gifts - specially designed chocolate boxes, intricate trinkets and bags and bags of tennis rackets - all with my face adorning their protective covers. They're using the photo of my first-round victory where I'm looking up at my wooden racket with a look of astonishment on my face. I'm not sure why they're using that one - there are many more with me in action on the court which would be much better images for the youth who will follow in my wake after this fortnight.

Amidst the tsunami of fan mail, severed horses' heads and indescribable underwear, I find the most satisfying emblem of my recent success: my local club have formulated a new youth policy in light of the hundreds of young children from near and afar who have come knocking on their doors, demanding to meet their local champion, expecting to breathe in the same air as he, and be honoured to share the same bar and curled up sandwiches on a Saturday afternoon.

My success, in short, has breathed new life into an ailing tennis section of an ossifying amateur sports club and the committee are now having to wake up to the realities of the 21st century.

And whilst of course nothing is guaranteed in this most frustrating of sports, what I am confident of is that my legacy on my local club cannot be ignored. Mrs Lady Chairman, the consistently dangerous grass surfaces, the warm keg beer, the disrespectful thirteen-year olds: these will all be things of the past when, at shortly after 4pm tomorrow afternoon, I lift up on high what is rightfully mine: the trophy of the Wimbledon Men's Singles Final.

We may not be a powerful tennis nation, but my story will inspire generations.

Like our glorious Olympic successes of 2012, it will lead to invigorated tennis policy in schools; to droves of happy families taking to their local courts over the weekends; and to a resurgent economy which catapults us back into the world as the leading economic powerhouse.

The future of empire has never looked so bright.

I AM ANDY MURRAY AND HAVE BEATEN ROGER FEDERER (ALBEIT VICARIOUSLY) (11–5)

Thank you thank you thank you thank you thank you thank you all. I can't believe that this afternoon has ended in such a thrilling style, with so many decisive moments, nerve tingling decisions, and life changing choices.

Novi was an incredible opponent this afternoon, but I agree with him when he says the best man won (i.e. me).

So, congratulations to him for putting up such a spirited fight, and congratulations to me for pulling out all the stops and astounding everyone.

While now is not the time to crow, it is worth remembering those who fell at an early stage during the competition and for the valuable contribution blah… blah… blah… they have made to the upper echelons of the tennis fraternity.

Holding the trophy aloft will stay in my memory for the rest of my life and I would like to finally thank you all, my supporters, my coach, my advocates and my enemies for the encouragement you have given me or the motivation which has spurred me on to prove you all wrong. This year's Wimbledon has proven to me that anything is possible, with the right attitude, guts, determination, and fertile imagination.

My club, my tennis, my world, will never be the same again.

Thank you thank you thank you thank you thank you thank you thank you thank you thank you thank you thank you thank you.

THIRD SET:
HOW TO BECOME
SPORTS
PERSONALITY OF
THE YEAR.

(FIRST SET: 2–6)
(SECOND SET: 11–5)

GUTTED. ROASTED. FUMING. (0-1)

You would have thought after all I have done - my surprise wild card entry to Wimbledon this year; my subsequent tussle for recognition with the guys in the locker room; my 'back-to-the-wall' heroic endeavours against the forces of bureaucratic inertia; my radical stance against Hawkeye, BBGs and the state of the grass; and ultimately the fact that I beat Novak Djokovic to become the first Englishman to win the Wimbledon Champions Final of 2013 at the All England Lawn Tennis and Croquet Club - you would have thought I would have merited at least a nomination in our club's Sports Personality of the Year Competition of the Year.

YOU WOULD HAVE THOUGHT!

You would have thought - having brought fame and recognition to our modest club; new generations of enthusiastic bright bushy tailed young tennis things to our courts; and sponsorship in the order of tens of pounds – you would have thought that the committee, in all its puffed up glory and self-importance, would have said to itself:

"Fair play. The boy done good. We shall take the extraordinary step of awarding him a special nomination that reflects his tremendous achievements."

But no. No such recognition is forthcoming.

I'm not disappointed about not receiving a nomination from the ordinary members - not in the least.

I understand how bitter and cynical and envious and aghast many of them felt at seeing my almost superhuman achievements over the summer. Their lack of respect for me now is a shame – but understandable. I would act in exactly the same way as them if I saw one of my peers plucked from middle-aged obscurity to a glistening future of signing tennis shorts, being interviewed by Russell Brand (my God, I was funny) and whining and dining with the likes of Princess Margot of Luxembourg and The Sheikh of Araby.

But the committee? They should know better and so are worthy of my most bilest of bile.

This is why.

As well as passively sitting back and just watching votes drift through their letterbox as and when the voter decides to pass by and exert their democratic duty, they have instituted an absolutely mind-boggling approach to local democracy. No longer is it enough, apparently, for the democratic process to be seen to be working. It must also be seen to be in need of repair, given that it is so obviously broken.

To this end, votes are not just added up and counted, they are judged and assessed by the committee members for their appropriateness. According to the committee, voters are clearly short of a few bob when it comes to their stocks of common sense in the voting department. They evidently need guidance as to who vote for. And if they don't make the right decision, then they need to have their vote adjusted to reflect what they really meant to say.

Not only that, but as well as being advised (or, dare I say, instructed) by the committee burghers to vote for the candidate of the burghers' choice, we are also being instructed to vote for a candidate OF THE OPPOSITE SEX – even if we have never come across any lady tennis players – or football players or rugby players or indeed any other activity which the Club deems to be sports like - in our time at the club.

And to cap it all – and this is the final straw that made me realise that Russell Brand is not a pouting show off with a mouth bigger than my tennis racket but a genuine democrat who has the health and wealth of this country at heart in all his media endeavours – the Committee, heaven help us, have decreed that voting shall be done in full view of all the committee members, AND instead of using a short stubby pencil as is usual in the Western Democratic process, we shall use our blood to mark an X on the ballot paper.

Rigged ballots? Directed voting? A mandate forged in blood?

These are not the signs of a healthy amateur tennis club but a wicked, corrupt and financially wayward nation whose last four letters end in -stan.

I have, needless to say, submitted my resignation from this once glorious community resource.

They may well have spurned me at the Annual General Meeting as well as the Dinner Dance, Gentlemen's Evening and subsequent Sports Personality of the Year but I am not bitter, not in any way, shape or form. Not a wit, not a jot. NA-DAL.

Speaking of which: Rafa has just called me for a game of mixed doubles with ladies from the tennis club across the park. I shall be delighted to join him and his grown-up compatriots and shall look to impart my wisdom hewn from the rocks of my 2013 Wimbledon's Men's Finals experience to their eager youth team.

I already sense a return visit to that august institution in 2014.

SPORTS PERSONALITY OF THE YEAR? "YOU'RE 'AVIN' A LARF." (0–2)

You, o wise, astute reader, will know the significance of what I am about to reveal as you are well versed in the trials and tribulations of village pump politics, bruised egos and sporty tantrums. None of which are mine I hasten to add.

You will also recognise, due to your hard won wisdom over the years, that my challenges have not been without merit, that my battles are of the most deserving kind, and that my stand against the forces of mediocrity and institutional inertia is a stand borne of optimistic idealism rather than one of self-serving, craven realpolitik.

I accept my idealism has sometimes been wayward, my optimism unwarranted and my belief in the underlying goodness of all humanity may have been misguided, but you - o wise, astute, and intelligent reader - will wave aside these flaws when it comes to assessing the rights and wrongs of the debacle that surrounded the so-called Sports Personality of the Year Awards Evening, and agree that I have been cruelly and unjustly treated in a year when, after all, I did win the 2013 Men's Singles Tennis Final at Wimbledon - the colossus of tennis tournaments.

There is no point beginning at the beginning. You will, because you have an excellent memory o wise, astute, intelligent and attractive reader, know that I won a wild card to Wimbledon. That I struggled against the collective might of the Balkan youth. That I was spurned, rejected and ridiculed by all the guys in the locker room. You will recall with great acuity how I made my way through all the qualifying rounds to the final. You will remember the final and you will know the result. The first British men's win at Wimbledon since Arnold Ffanshawe succeeded - against much lesser opposition - in 1808.

You will also be aghast – as I was – at the terrible snubbing I received at the hands of the sub-humans who make up our so-called club committee when I was left off the list of nominations for the Sports Personality Of The Year competition.

Now, like you, o wise, astute, intelligent, attractive and mature reader, I took this news on the chin and reacted magnanimously.

I resigned with immediate effect and took my racket and Wimbledon balls to the club down the road where I promptly joined their august institution, and where I have been happy ever since.

Except. I didn't. And I haven't.

To be honest, o wise, astute, intelligent, attractive, mature, and fun-loving reader, I took the news very badly. I yearned to be on the short list. I hungered to be acknowledged as the immense tennis player I am. I would have given my left non-serving arm to have even been invited to the evening. But my coach, Hac, advised against this sacrifice claiming it would jeopardise my ranking in the world's elitist of the elite.

But the fact is, o wise, astute, intelligent, attractive, mature, fun loving, and sympathetic reader, I didn't get a look in. Not one call, not one email, not one text. Nothing.

So here I am, nose pressed against the window of the grand room of what was my former club looking in at the cavorting that is going on inside, all in the name of praising so-called 'sports personalities'.

I see huge turkeys, stuffed with chickens, themselves stuffed with quails which in turn are stuffed with baby pigeons paraded around the dance floor - not live I hasten to add, but cooked to roasted perfection. I hear tarantellas, waltzes, minuets - all played to within an inch of their lives - and see committee members dressed up in their Christmas finery, adorned with hats in the shape of tennis rackets, rugby union posts, referee whistles, any number of sports accessories masquerading as the highest of high sports fashion.

But where are the achievers, I hear you ask, o wise, astute, intelligent, attractive, mature, fun loving, sympathetic, and discerning reader? Where are the signs of achievement? The true victors of the summer? And you would be well to ask such important questions.

The answer is here in front of you.

He is here, shivering in the icy cold, wearing his Fred Perry singlet and Rafa Nadal shorts and Roger Federer golden trainers (the ones with RF17 embossed in golden thread on the ankles) and asking himself, "why, oh! why?"

And I know dear reader, that you are unable to answer being the club cat that you are.

You stare at me; I stare at you. You miaow; I for once am speechless. I can't let you in. I am the committee blocking your entrance to the not so great and not so good. The world needs spirits such as us o wise, astute, intelligent, attractive, mature, fun loving, sympathetic, discerning, and feline listener. The trouble is, it doesn't know it yet.

Sports Personality Of The Year? From now on I shall call you, the club moggie, Spoty. Your secret is safe with me.

SPORTS PERSONALITY OF THE YEAR? MOI? (1–2)

I awoke on the dew drenched field of my alma mater this morning with a headache the size of Concorde. Clutching my tennis racket firmly to my Fred Perry adorned bosom, I realised in the vicious light of day that it was all over, once and for all, between me and the club. Not on the short list of SPOTY, no invite to the awards ceremony, not even a half-eaten chicken thrown my way out of sympathy.

How the mighty are fallen.

Even the club moggie had deserted me I mused as I trudged out of the ground. But such is the way of all things feline and racket shaped. They may love you when you're up there – struggling, winning, bathing in the showers afterwards – but when you're down and out, flat on your back on a dew drenched rugby field? Then you realise who your real friends are.

And Spoty, the club moggie is clearly not one of them.

But – and this is a big but – one that combines all the *'on the other hands'*, *'howevers'* and *'they think it's all overs'* that are possible in any sports mythology, including mine – what did I see as I slumped past the newsagent this morning? On his bill board? Written in thick black felt tip marker?

Only the short list for the BBC's Sports Personality Of The Year 2013 programme!

And who is on THAT list, alongside Mo Farah, Christine Ohuruogu, Hannah Cockroft, Chris Froome, Justin Rose, Sir (Sir!) Ben Ainslie, AP McCoy, Ian Bell and rugby union player Leigh Halfpenny? Yes, that's right - little old moi!

Yours truly has been recognised by the true sporting elite and is there in the public eye once again despite being snubbed by the cultural pygmies of his own club!

The public will vote for their favourite on Sunday, 15 December – giving me just a few weeks to practice my personality so that it stands the best possible chance of success.

Sports Personality Of The Year?

Last night you may have been 'avin a larf, but this morning is a very different place in the sports cosmos and I for one intend to claim what is rightfully mine.

Spoty – club moggie – and all you club apparatchiks – you have been warned.

PRACTICING MY PERSONALITY FOR SPOTY (2-2)

Since hearing about my nomination on the BBC's Sports Personality Of The Year 2013, I have become a new man.

Whilst the broadcast is not until 17 December on the world's most prestigious TV channel, BBC1, I realise I need to get into some serious training in order to beat off the fierce competition.

Fail to prepare and prepare to fail; no pain no gain; you gotta be in it to win it; every dog has its day; go smash the opposition and stand victorious over the entrails with their heads on pikes on railings on Tower Bridge and rub your hands in glee at their miserable fortunes.

I am remembering all the wise words of tennis wisdom that have adorned the world's most prestigious of tennis centre - Wimbledon. Where I won this year's men's singles finals, in case you forgot or have been asleep for the last six months.

But I am aware too that SPOTY 2013 (as it is affectionately referred to in the world's most prestigious corridors of power in Westminster) is not just a test of sporting prowess but one which measures, assesses and judges one's PERSONALITY.

I am only too well aware that last year I was ridiculed for having a very short supply of aforesaid attribute. People – ignorant, cowardly people, truth be told – said I was brusque. Rude beyond compare. Had the personality of a rubber duck. Should never have been in the studio never mind on the short list.

But this year will be different.

The time for the rubber duck to show his true colours has come - as indeed I knew it would.

And it will be different for one very good reason. I shall be practicing my personality with the same care and devotion that I practice my tennis backhand, overhead smash, net leaping and raising aloft of my Thunderhammer Thor mark 6.1 tennis weapon. This will involve beaming at other people; cheering when one of my tennis 'colleagues' flukes a point on a net call and sitting in the bar after an intense afternoon of fierce but friendly competition quaffing Hawkeye by the yard.

My personality will be fit and honed by 17 December and whilst I am clearly not a shoe-in to SPOTY (some of my competitors are the world's most prestigious athletes after all. The fact that a lot of them sit down whilst undertaking their sport – mentioning no names Sir (Sir!) Ben Kingsley- is immaterial), the indisputable fact is that the British TV audience – the world's most prestigious TV audience, incidentally – know a winner when they see one.

And I shall be up there. Mark my words.

WHAT EXACTLY IS A 'SPORTS PERSONALITY?' (3-2)

In the hours that have elapsed since the announcement of the short list of this year's Sports Personality Of The Year tournament on the BBC, I have devoted myself to the job in hand of ensuring that as well as winning the men's finals at this year's Wimbledon, I am in the best possible position to waltz off with this prestigious prize from our most prestigious of broadcasters. This has involved an assessment of my opponents' personality strengths and weaknesses (especially their weaknesses, of course) so that I can mount a suitably effective public campaign to ensure that the prize comes to its natural home: the shelf above my fireplace.

My opponents' weaknesses are legion.

Mo Farah and Christine Ohuruogu are both runners and we all know that runners exhibit no personality whatsoever due to the inane nature of their sport. Running around and around in circles? Sometimes for hours on end? Without deviation, hesitation or repetition (as my good friend Nicholas Parsons would have chided them, had they had the wit to make their running career the slightest bit interesting)? Puh-leeese.

Clearly, whilst both good eggs who did their bit for our recent Olympic effort, both Mo and Christine are out of the depth when it comes to exhibiting the strength of character needed to succeed at the highest of sporting pinnacles.

Which would be – in case you missed it – the men's singles finals at Wimbledon this year.

Which I won – in case you were in any doubt.

Hannah Cockroft and Chris Froome suffer from a similar complaint. They both pursue their sporting activities with the advantage of a bicycle. This clearly gives them an unfair edge over the unfortunate Mo and Christine who use their legs for most of their time on the track. Hannah and Chris also depend on the bicycle saddle to sit down on for their sport – to sit down on! - which suggests some serious character flaws that will mean their personalities quickly unravel in the heat of the television studio moment. Not ones to register on the threat scale, methinks.

Likewise, Justin Rose, AP McCoy (who he?) and Ian Bell can all be regarded as also-rans in the tournament, given that a) no-one called Justin has ever had a personality, b) no-one has ever heard of AP McCoy (who he?) and c) Ian Bell's personality is probably quite charming, but given his genealogy, is probably a raving demon the rest of the time and not fit to grace any TV studio at any time of year, never mind when the SPOTY Tournament is in full flow.

That leaves Sir (Sir!) Ben Ainslie (who sits down to play his sport) and rugby union player Leigh Halfpenny who I think are the most likely challengers for what is rightfully mine.

I have become acutely aware of the power of royalty in the public sphere so anyone with Sir in front of their name is likely to make a huge impression on the public consciousness before breakfast time. Likewise, Leigh Halfpenny – despite having a name to be ridiculed – is to be taken ultra-seriously given his ability to crush an opponent to smithereens as soon as look at him.

These two may or may not constitute serious challenges to the title of Sports Personality Of The Year – but I know I will need to tread carefully when it comes to engaging in battle with them. One could summon up the forces of the monarchy against me; the other could ensure I never trod on Gods good earth ever again.

These are serious personalities for serious times.

HOW TO MOUNT A CHARM OFFENSIVE (3-3)

It's comforting to know that the early signs from the bookmakers are that I shall probably walk the prestigious Sports Personality Of The Year 2013 tournament on 17 December. My opposition – if that's what you call it – is already lagging a long way behind me in the personality stakes due to three critical factors I have detected since the short list was announced. These are simply charm, charm and more charm.

Let me explain, charmingly.

The first lesson in persuading the public of one's substantial personality and gravitas is to find every opportunity to charm your way into their hearts through the use of the media, your neighbours and your fiercest enemies - in my case, the doughty committee of my local club who, surprise surprise, have still not yet summoned up the grace to make contact with me on hearing that I was not only on the BBC shortlist but ahead by a country mile.

Dealing with the press has been a straightforward enough affair. I have a database of every single tin pot journalist on the local rag and follow them avidly on twitter, email them regularly with my latest movements, and phone them when they least expect it with news from my campaign headquarters. I brief them discreetly, regularly and anonymously and I have favourites to whom I drop tasty morsels about my whereabouts, intentions, opinions, shopping lists, contents of my litter bins and mobile phone PIN numbers so that they can have no excuse not to hack me and find out every salacious detail of my private life. Thus, am I guaranteed to be 'up there' with the best of the rest of them when it comes to attracting their attention.

Jude Law, Alan Partridge and Hugh Grant have all learnt a thing or two from me about how to garner press interest, I can tell you.

My neighbours are somewhat less difficult to persuade of the merits of my qualification for the tournament. When I approach them in the car park, knock on their doors last thing at night, or leave them alone until they look like they're ready to engage in conversation at the local Sainsbury's, most of them seem to feign memory loss, and struggle to remember who I am, why I am talking at them and what they need to do before D Day of 17 December. This perplexes me as I have known many of them for years and we have always seemed to get on well when we pass each other in the corridor or on the stair well. But such is the way of the world. When the sun rises on the morning of 18 December, I know who will be knocking on whose door and who will be the first to offer mince pies and glasses of sherry to sports personalities of international stature dressed in their pyjamas.

The committee though is another kettle of carp.

Still ignorant in its ways, still rude in its manner and yet still just a bit out of reach. I am convinced that if I can persuade just one member of the committee to cast their vote for me by phone on or before 17 December, the nature of the beast is such that before long the whole flock of them will be dialling the BBC ready to do the necessary. With that will come recognition of my achievements: invitations to Boxing Day lunches, nominations to join the fund-raising subcommittee and dare I whisper it? Eventual leadership of the club itself. Yes, there, I've said it.

The Chairmanship.

That is what is at stake after 17 December and whilst winning the most prestigious sporting trophy in the world is not something to be sniffed at, it pales into insignificance with the main prize.

The Chairmanship.

The parking space in the car park. The seat at the bar. The dimpled tankard out of which one would sup gallons of Hawkeye until one would fall over and be levered into one's car by the trusty security guard. These are the things dreams are made of.

Say it loud, say it soft, just say it like Homer Simpson... 'Chair...Man...Ship' and you will sense the allure of the task ahead.

HOW TO DEAL WITH THE RUMOUR MILL THAT IS THE INTERNATIONAL TENNIS CIRCUIT (4–3)

I hadn't heard from Ilie for over a year, so imagine my surprise if you can when I opened my email this morning to find an invitation from him to play in a world rankings tournament in Oman this afternoon. It wasn't the destination or the short notice that was the surprise but the fact that he remembered me at all. He's got a poor memory has Mr Nastase.

But there's no getting away from the fact that he's still a canny player when he puts his distracted mind to it. We had a fierce tussle on court trading grimace for grimace, grunt for grunt, and deft power half-volley base line shot (me) with tricksy wrist action back hand (him). The peak came in the 14th game when we battled out a six-point rally. Which I won, naturally.

So all is well in the tennis universe apart from the fact that Mr Nastase also let slip in a typical absent minded moment that whilst everyone in the locker room thought it was inevitable that I would be winning next week's Sports Personality Of The Year 2013 competition, there was a distinct left of field tendency in some of my old opponents to mount a scurrilous campaign which would lead me being pipped to the tennis post by another sweaty candidate on the SPOTY shortlist: and one who sits down to play his sport to boot, namely Sir (Sir!) Ben Kingsley.

I laughed off his absent-minded rumour and dismissed it as the meanderings of a man who has spent far too long in the locker rooms of the planet with or without various assorted, unnamed and unattributable acquaintances. But the thought niggled away at me whilst we showered.

Sir (Sir!) Ben Kingsley?

Has more personality than me?

I resolved to fly back to the UK immediately and get on the blower to my fan base to ensure the wheels weren't coming off my campaign. And if Sir (Sir!) Ben Kingsley was anywhere to be detected in this dastardly plot then I would be up to the BBC immediately to lodge the necessary litigation. He may have had a bit part in Gandhi; he may have excelled in Iron Man Three – but as a sportsman who sits on a boat and sails around and around the Isle of Wight a few times and expects to snatch the highly lauded SPOTY prize of SPOTY prizes away from its rightful owner?

I think not.

I sent Ilie Nastase back to his village in Transylvania with one message for the troublemakers of the locker rooms: back off. SPOTY 2013 is to be mine. All mine.

I'M SPOTY! NO, I'M SPOTY! WHY IS SPOTY BECOMING MORE LIKE SPARTACUS EVERY DAY? (5-3)

The proliferation of SPOTY awards that seem to have crept out of the skirting boards over the last 24 hours is getting beyond a joke.

No sooner is the premiere brand announced – SPOTY 2013 on the BBC on 17 December in case you really haven't kept up in recent weeks – than a host of other SPOTY awards appear on the media hillside.

Young SPOTY, Old SPOTY and Stripy SPOTY have all appeared out of nowhere and it's really quite exasperating having to contend with not only the members of the very important short list on which I am a front runner, but all these other infernal lists as well.

What on earth do they think they're playing at, these PR gurus who have jumped on the SPOTY bandwagon waving media clip boards like apaches down at the OK Corral on the old East End Road on a Saturday night? Do they really think they are celebrating the achievements of us toughened up professionals who have fought hand over fist to get on TV that evening?

Do they not appreciate what it takes to win the Wimbledon's Men's Tennis Final 2013 against all the odds?

Where were they when I was up against it? Were they heralding the rise of the underdog back in the summer when I was taking on the committee, the Balkan Youth and sundry tennis champions singlehandedly with merely an old wooden Dunlop in one hand and a pint of Hawkeye in the other?

"Were they 'eck 's like!" as they say in the Lady Chairman's native Barnsley.

They were ignoring my progress until the morning after the afternoon before, and now, all of a sudden, they think they can commemorate any old Tim, Dirk or Betty for their measly attempts to jump over a bar which is marginally higher than their knee caps. And they even have a mattress to land on when they reach the other side these so called high jumpers! If they were real athletes, they'd jump as high as they could unaided and risk breaking their backs on their return to earth.

That would give them something to be SPOTY about.

LIVING THE LIFE OF REILLY WITH GRACE DISPENSING FAVOURS (6-3)

So here I am, sat on the veranda of my penthouse luxury suite on the Thames, clutching my SPOTY 2013 trophy in my right hand and my Wimbledon Singles Tournament Men's Champion Final urn in the other.

Behind me, quaffing champagne and endless supplies of Hawkeye bitter are the highest of the highest of the glitterati and celeberati. Sir (Sir!) Ben Kingsley has just parked up on the jetty below in his sailor's dinghy and waved to me with a traditional maritime greeting of respect, the two fingered salute made famous by the one and only Winston Churchill whose grandson, Winston Winston Winston Churchill, dropped by not five minutes ago to collect the rent.

In my kitchen, the world's political elite are arguing over global warming, economic meltdown and the recent death of Lou Reed. As far as I know, Lou never lifted a tennis racket in his life, although a little bird in the shape of Hannah Cockroft no less, tells me he was party to a lot more racketeering than he would have had us believe.

But tonight, after this glorious success of all successes, surpassed only by…. Well, surpassed by nothing actually, tonight has just taken the biscuit.

Mine is not to reason why, count the cost or favour, fortune or fight anyone on any beaches anywhere. Mine is to lap it all up, big style.

I have to admit (no, really, I do) to feeling some moments of sympathy for my unlucky rivals in this year's SPOTY competition (which I won by the way, just in case you didn't know). AP McCoy (who he?) is still trying to get people to recognise him and is floating from guest to guest at my party, trying to persuade them that they really do know him – or would do if they had been following the results of the 2.15 at Uttoxeter on that last rainy Bank Holiday Monday.

Leigh 'Weatherspoon' Halfpenny has rendered himself a few pennies short of the full shilling tonight in the only way that rugby players know – by the downing of vast quantities of vodka followed by the obligatory tossing of each other into the River Thames. Disgusting behaviour for a supposed 'personality' never mind a SPOTY for 2013!

Chris Froome has taken himself off in a huff and is sitting on the kitchen barstool, his legs going round and round furiously in vain - he's getting nowhere. You can take the boy off the bike, but you can't take the bike out of the boy as Stephen Gerrard reliably informed me when we shared a bowl of twiglets together.

Mo Farah and Christine Ohuruogu have continued to do what they do best: run around in ever-decreasing circles ad infinitum until everybody has developed neck pains watching them.

There's no getting away from it: in order to win the most prestigious sports competition in the world, the Sports Personality Of The Year, on the world's most prestigious broadcaster, the wonderful BBC1, one needs to have a bucket load of personality.

And that ladies and gentlemen, is why I, the Soon-to-be-Lord Andrew John Paul George Ringo Murray of Kirkintilloch, have secured the prize in such emphatic style.

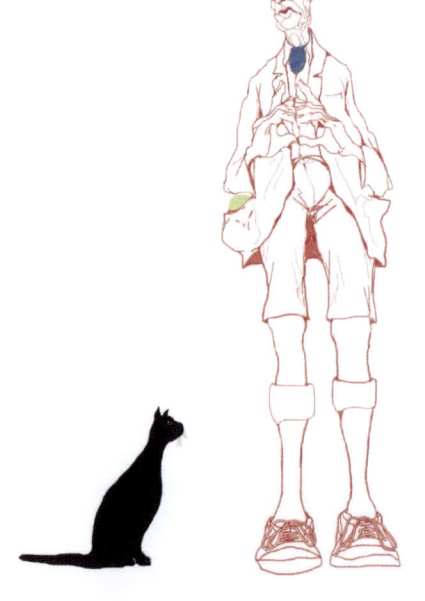

Now there is only one thing left to complete my universe. Recognition of my achievements by my local club, which has, as you can imagine, been less than effusive in its praise in recent weeks.

No matter. The time is now right for the club secretary, Grace, to phone me and inform me that the club is ready to bestow the ultimate accolade upon me.

The Chairmanship.

Grace, I am ready for your favours.

FOURTH SET:
HOW TO WIN
POWER,
AUTHORITY AND
INFLUENCE.

(FIRST SET: 2–6)
(SECOND SET: 11–5)
(THIRD SET: 6–3)

WAITING FOR MY MAN (0-1)

The man in question, dear reader, is, as you know, the Chair-man-ship of my old lawn tennis club with whom I have had a long standing attachment – might one say love hate relationship or hate hate relationship if you were the churlish club tennis captain – over many years (3 to be precise) and to whom I have bought fame, fortune and bar takings.

I am waiting for the aforesaid man to be offered to me in recognition of my breath-taking achievements this year, which, if you didn't know have been a) winning a wild card to Wimbledon, b) winning all my matches at Wimbledon against all the odds, c) winning the final itself against Novak Djokovich, d) being nominated for the BBC Sports Personality Of The Year (SPOTY) competition and e) winning the aforesaid competition, against all the odds, expectations and any reasonable human judgement.

So. The next logical step is for Grace, the club secretary, to phone me and inform me of the ruminations of the club committee, tell me which way the ashes blew out of the smoke stack above the squash courts, and invite me to discreetly attend an informal meeting over best foaming Hawkeye beer and skittles, at which, in the best club tradition, I would be sounded out over my availability and interest in the roles of Executive President, Chief Executive Officer, Chairman and Honorary Saint, in gratitude for the overwhelming good I have bestowed upon the club in the time I have graced its courts.

But. So far, so no phone call.

My Thames penthouse suite is deserted after the revels of the last forty-eight hours. Lesser sportsmen have returned to their playing fields to practice their personalities and prepare for the next encounter with their opponents - who will no doubt be seething with envy for these upstarts' exposure on prime time BBC1.

A few scores will be settled in the coming days on the playing fields of Caerphilly, the roads of Dagenham and the Birmingham Bullring.

The politicians have scampered back to their second houses, the film stars returned to their caravans, Michael Bublé has plugged himself into the mains down in the basement as his batteries were running out. And I am left here alone, staring at the phone, waiting for my man.

SPEECHLESS IN STRATHCLYDE (0–2)

Imagine my excitement. Now the thrills and spills of SPOTY are over, my London pad has been taken back by its landlord, Winston Winston Winston Churchill, some heir apparent of the great chieftain himself, by his own account, although you would never have guessed it by looking at the rather shabby Ford Cortina he drove up the drive in.

So I hot foot it back to the 'shires to be met by my faithful valet on the station platform and I'm whisked away to a secret location before any paparazzi can get wind of my latest moves.

Over a bottle of the finest single malt from a secluded distillery in the heart of the Borders, I sit and wait for the phone to ring.

I wait all day. Nothing happens. And all night. Nothing happens.

Undeterred, I wait longer, missing my customary breakfast of Scots Porridge Oats smothered in Highland Glen Honey and Lothian Yoghurt.

Until 11.03am precisely when the phone rings. I answer it.

It's Grace from the Club.

My prayers and my patience have been answered. They – the Committee (the Committee!) – would like to meet me for an informal meeting. As soon as possible. Today even! I feign disinterest but deep inside I am chomping at the proverbial tennis bit and can't wait to slip on my plus fours, shooting jacket and deer stalker hat and tear through the countryside in my old jalopy to park myself on their lawns, enter the clubhouse and nonchalantly accept their carefully worded offer of the permanent Chairmanship of their (my!) illustrious club.

For what seems an eternity, I find myself sat waiting in a flea-bitten yellowing armchair outside Grace's office. The big Clubhouse clock ticks ominously. The door squeaks open and a disconnected hand beckons me inside. Facing me are the full twelve members of the Committee in all their crusty glory. Banksey. Gladhand. Butchers Dog. Freddie Flintoff. Serena Pinkington Ffanshawe Blingworthy. Seasick Steve. Fiona 1. Fiona 2. Big fat red faced man whose name I can never remember. Troll. The Chairman, the Right Reverend MP Gingerbread Man. And of course, the secretary, Grace.

"It has come to our attention…" begins the Chairman in time honoured tradition. He was always a stickler for protocol, and I admire him enormously for it.

"It has come to our attention…." Yes, yes, get on with it, I think, get on and tell me you have recognised my immense achievements in the last six months and are about to reward me accordingly by stepping down and elevating me to your hallowed seat.

"It has come to our attention that you, sir, have failed to pay your membership subscription for the last three years – in fact, ever since you arrived here – and that you have been playing on our courts in a manner which is against both the terms and conditions of this club's membership and the spirit of lawn tennis in general. We would like an explanation and preferably a cheque backdated to 2010 covering your debt to us."

You, dear, respected, intelligent and sympathetic reader, will appreciate the level of aghastness I felt on hearing these slurs against my character, not least the obvious omission in his introductory paragraphs. They have called me in to pay my so called 'subs'.

Me!

The soon-to-be Lord Andrew John Paul George Ringo Murray of Kirkintillock is expected to pay a so called 'subscription'! Going back three years to the time I joined the institution!

I didn't know where to look or what to say, with all those gnarled faces staring at me, up at the ceiling, or out of the window. I had no option but to beat a hasty retreat back to the jalopy, my reputation in tatters and my bank account under attack.

Wimbledon Men's Singles Tournament Final Champion. Winner of the BBC SPOTY competition of 2013. But publicly disgraced and financially embarrassed member of the county's Premiere Tennis Club?

Most certainly not. Clearly the Club Chairmanship was proving to be as elusive as ever and I needed to take steps to protect my reputation. There was only one thing for it.

Bring on Roger Federer.

BROKE, BATTERED BUT NOT YET BEATEN (0-3)

For rent: tennis superstar available for after dinner lectures, gentlemen's nights and bar mitzvahs… For sale: tennis legend going cheap, all genuine offers considered…. BOGOF: tennis world champion now taking bookings for winter training sessions…

I have to say – no, really, I do – that things aren't looking great. My recent humiliation at the hands of the accursed committee and their dastardly suggestion that I was behind with my 'subs' as they call it has laid me lower than low.

One might think if one was unversed in the ways of tennis superstardom (probably like you, dear reader) that the tiny matter of a few hundred pounds subscription to a lower than low league tennis club would not cause the likes of myself too much concern.

"You must have made millions since your Wimbledon triumph," you might reasonably suggest. But the fact is, the lifestyle of the Wimbledon winner is a far cry from the commonly held belief that life is a bowl of champagne floating on an iceberg of lovely ladies who pander to your every physical and mental desire.

On the contrary, the financial demands are immense. There are Bentleys to book, Michelin star chefs to placate and fans underwear to return. All take their financial toll. So, contrary to what you might expect, I am now brassic. Down to my last – well actually my valet's – last shekel. Which is why I have taken the unholy step of prostituting myself around the county circuit and offering my wit and tennis expertise to anybody who will pay.

A few postcards in the off-licence window haven't yet done the trick but I suspect that this is more due to seasonal pressures than it is my lack of marketability. But copywriter I am not: so dear reader, if you could see yourself to penning a few winning sentences which would raise me the necessary lucre to pay my 'subs' I would be much obliged.

Now, back to the typewriter…

TV superstar seeks winning partner… GSOH essential.

iANDREW MURRAY LTD IS NOT A FIGMENT OF YOUR IMAGINATION (1-3)

Who would have thought it?

Me, soon to be Lord Andrew John Paul George Ringo Murray of Kirkintilloch slumming it with the hoi polloi down at the local job centre with a rag tag and bob tail collection of down at heel window cleaners, dog groomers and dot com wannabes who claim to have reinvented Google from a ditch in their allotment?

Truth is. dear reader, my efforts to raise the necessary bitcoinage to pay for my 'subscription' at my tennis club which would entitle me to claim what's rightfully mine i.e. the Tennis Club Chairmanship are floundering.

Postcard ads in the post office window generated precisely nothing. Begging letters to long forgotten friends and family likewise. Shaking a can at the pensioners in the high street (well, the ones who can't walk away too quickly) with a doleful expression on my face leads to insults about Eastern European migrants taking our jobs, homes, school places and tennis championship titles.

So, I have resorted to the worst of all possible worlds: I have joined a course which claims it is going to make an entrepreneur out of me and enable, encourage and force me to make a new 'business' (dread word!) out of the meagre resources I can scrape together - which as you know, dear reader, are limited to my Wimbledon urn and SPOTY gift voucher.

If you had told me six months ago that I would be reduced to selling Andy Murray merchandise to struggling farmers' markets around the Borders or aggressive distributors in the South Bronx I would have dismissed your suggestion with a dismissive forehand volley deep to the back of your backhand baseline. But as life has turned out, that is exactly what these so called 'trainers' on this so called 'programme' are enabling, encouraging and forcing me to think about with something resembling an air of menacing threat behind their shiny beaming smiles.

They suggested I start with a so called 'SWOT' analysis. I told them I knew all about swatting tennis balls around the tennis court and had the Wimbledon urn to prove it. But they were having none of it: SWOT analysis they explained in words of no more than one syllable was a tool to understand what I was, was not, should be sad about and should be glad about.

This didn't take long. Strengths? Too many to list. Weaknesses? Too few to care about. Opportunities? Threats? In my game I retorted opportunities and threats were two sides of the same imposter – namely the whole wide world – and the sooner one got to grips with that, the better.

So my SWOT analysis was a mercifully short document which led to my creation of iAndrew Murray Ltd: one share holder (yours truly) selling a range of authentic tennis related merchandise endorsed by one international tennis superstar (yours truly). My website was created in a matter of seconds and now my business is ready for action.

Lord Andrew John Paul George Ringo Murray of Kirkintilloch International Jet Setting Sporting Olympian, Media Darling, and now Leading-Edge Entrepreneur?

Remember, you heard it here first.

Come to me, o chairmanship, your wait to be handed over to your rightful owner is nearly over.

GOD BLESS ROGER FEDERER AND ALL WHO SAIL IN HIM (2-3)

There's no denying it - it takes one elite sportsman to recognise another and support them in their time of need.

Form is temporary but class is permanent, as many a wise owl has noted in things pertaining to the sports arena, and Roger Federer is clearly one who has enough class and is big hearted enough to know when to pay his dues to his elders and betters, particularly when times are tough.

Today just one solitary envelope popped through my letter box. I recognised the untidy handwriting immediately. It was Roger doing his best to write by joining up his letters and writing in a straight line. I tore open the envelope and out dropped six postal orders which amounted to the debt I was alleged to have accrued at the club.

There was a small Christmas card too with a picture of a mountain horn bedecked with sprigs of holly, but I dismissed this error of taste as being symptomatic of one who had spent too much formative time in his youth herding goats on mountains.

My next steps immediately became clear.

I would cash the postal orders, head straight down to the club, place the cash dramatically on the club bar in full view of the crinkly committee members who would be fused to their leather arm chairs, and demand a membership card, a copy of the constitution and a full public apology from all my detractors.

There might even be enough change to order a couple of swift pints of Hawkeye whilst enacting my revenge.

The plan went like a dream: everything fell into place exactly as I had planned, and to cap it all, I was able to decipher from the constitution that the next AGM would be on Wednesday 1 January 2014: and that nominations for the chairmanship would be open until Christmas Eve.

My destiny was now clearly in my hands: if I was to secure my goal of goals I would have to nominate myself, find a seconder, submit the paperwork by 24 December, lobby like crazy over the holiday period and then turn up on 1 January to reap the reward of my efforts.

I realised I had no time to waste: I had to get the nomination papers to Roger F. collect his signature and hotfoot it back to the club. I had no doubt that Roger would oblige and true to form he signed the forms in triplicate using his gold embossed Osmiroid.

Before you could say SPOTY 2014, all my ducks were in a line and my final challenge of 2013 was in my cross wires. All I need to do now is stoke up support for my nomination and sit back and watch my supporters descend on the club in their hoards, swamping the tennis club's letter box with votes for me.

The committee may well have not deemed it necessary to invite me to become their chairman: but after I had mobilised my tanks onto their well-manicured lawn tennis grass courts, they would realise what a dire mistake they had made.

Roger Federer, I salute you. Even though I did beat you (albeit vicariously) in the 3rd round of Wimbledon 2013.

ANDY – RAFA – NOVI – SERENA? WHO YOU GONNA CALL? CLUB MEMBERS! (3-3)

Well dear, true and faithful reader - you, who have been with me every step of the way over the tumultuous last six months, who have lived my lows, 'high fived' my highs (as they say in the locker room), and sympathetically shared my anguish and torture at the hands of imbeciles - you dear, trusted and discerning reader (and voter too at the tennis club if I'm not very much mistaken!) know what today brings and what it augurs for tomorrow.

You will know, dear reader – as I have it on good authority that you are a fully paid up member of the club – that you will be called upon to do your duty in the coming days. And I'm not just referring to increasing the bar takings or reducing the death rate on the squash courts: these are trivial matters in the grand scheme of things.

I'm referring to the very existence of the club and the person on whose shoulders that enormous responsibility should rest for the future.

Dear, wise and inscrutable reader, you are faced I now know with some very difficult decisions at the forthcoming AGM on 1 January. Whilst I never thought it would be a foregone conclusion that I would be an obvious choice for the role of Chairman of the club, I was not prepared for the competition it has generated.

To cut a very long story short, not only am I, the soon-to-be-Lord Andrew John Paul George Ringo Murray of Kirkintilloch on the shortlist of potential Chairman – but I have been joined in my hunt for the role by the combined forces of Rafa 'Riff-raff' Nadal, Novak 'Novi' Djokovic and the esteemed Mrs Serena 'Bolshie' Williams. Quite why she has applied for the ChairMANship is utterly beyond me but we'll let that pass for the moment.

So, pragmatic yet visionary, responsible yet free-spirited, accountable yet independent, and individual yet team player reader, your future – the future of the club – the future of the local economy – the future of English tennis – my future – is in your hands.

I trust you understand the term "x marks the spot" when it comes to placing your short stubby pencil on the ballot paper next week and will have no difficulty in putting your precious mark against the letters M U R R A Y, A.

Under club rules, all nominees now have to go into purdah for the week and are allowed no form of lobbying whatsoever. One might unreasonably dispute such a ridiculous rule but being a reasonable sort of Chairman-in-waiting, I shall do no such thing and will let the democratic process take it's due and unhindered course towards its natural and obvious decision.

If in the meantime, you would like an informal clarification of my policies, I shall be ensconced in the club bar every day now for the next week. All drinks are on me and if you wish, I will be able to offer you generous discounts on my solar powered Andy Murray action figure. It wields a tennis racket whilst simultaneously downing a miniature pint of Hawkeye in one swift movement and would make an excellent Christmas or New Year present for your nearest and dearest.

In the meantime, just remember who you're gonna call:

M U R R A Y, A. X

WHY RAFA NADAL IS NOT GOING TO MAKE IT (4–3)

Whilst we nominees for the Club Chairmanship are in purdah until 31 December and technically not allowed to lobby or promote our cause in any way whatsoever, there is nothing in the rules which prevents us from answering questions from voters who are rightly concerned about their future of their local club and English tennis in general.

So, when I, the soon-to-be-Lord Andrew John Paul George Ringo Murray of Kirkintilloch am asked by earnest bespectacled young players who sidle up to me in the bar about why they should not give their vote to any of my competitors – Rafa 'Riff-raff' Nadal, Novak 'Novi' Djokovic and the esteemed Mrs Serena 'Bolshie' Williams – I have no choice but to address their concerns in as honest and as balanced a manner as I can muster. It would, after all, be rude not to.

So, for those of you who are considering placing your X against the name of Rafa Nadal, I would point to his record of playing away during our recent long hot summer and ask that you ask yourself this: is he a man who deserves my hard won democratic vote? Especially after his irritating habit of planting himself on the passenger seat of other people's cars at the end of a tournament?

Does Rafa not possess a car of his own you might ask? Which would be a very good question indeed, opening up as it does various questions about the state of his driving licence, such as: does he have one? If not, why not? Might it be because he has failed his driving test at least sixteen times and only possesses the Spanish equivalent of our Cycling Proficiency Test? Or, if he does have a licence, how many speeding points does it show? And if none, is this because he had to send the original paper copy back to the Spanish DVLA in order to wipe off the string of offences which made his licence look like a carriage of a subway train from the Bronx?

And even if his licence does demonstrate a good and upstanding character, is his desire to hitchhike his way around the world's tennis clubs a sign of a player who is perhaps struggling to rub a few Euros together? Who has perhaps blown his substantial personal fortune on all kinds of fripperies which can be best summed up in the words wine, women and song? (And perhaps not in that order?)

As you know dear reader, I am not one to harbour malicious feelings against fellow Olympian athletes and certainly not one to spread unfounded and unattributable rumours, however plausible they might sound. But in the case of one Mr. Señor Rafael Jesus Hernandez Alfredo don Quixote de Nadal, I only can offer you one recommendation should you choose to wave your vote in his general direction on 1 January: clamp your car wheels if you don't want to lose it to this most persuasive of nominal Club chairmen-in-waiting.

WHY NOVAK DJOKOVICH IS NOT GOING TO MAKE IT (5-3)

Now, I have the utmost respect for Mr. Novak 'Novi' Djokovich and everything he has achieved on the tennis circuit. He has been, without doubt, a supreme men's singles tennis player. However, not many people know this, but his unacknowledged area of expertise is the mixed-doubles circuit, on which he has shown astounding tennis nous, albeit with a puzzling long string of female accomplices, none of whom stay with him for more than a couple of rubbers.

I have never been able to work out why this is but his achievements are without question and I doff my cap to him and all he has sailed in.

But the clue as to why is not a fit and proper person to lead our esteemed club is, I am sorry to say, down to his mental stability.

It is no coincidence that Novak Djokovich is frequently mistaken for his alter ego, Djovak 'Doli' Nokovich. This is because dear Noli's memory is failing badly and has been for some considerable time. He not only doesn't remember his own name anymore, but he has also taken to losing the club's weekly playing subscriptions, an affliction which has seen us lose over £19,973.95 this year alone.

Now, I'm not saying that Novi is light fingered or that he has any designs on our club's substantial assets and bank balances. Far from it. Novi has been generous to a double fault ever since he won his first major. The bigger question is whose assets has he been generous with? This has remained a major silence in our club and one which his manifesto – which I have here in front of me, pinned to the club dartboard – fails to answer.

So, following the club rules which state that all nominees for the club chairmanship are not allowed to lobby prior to the AGM on 1 January, I adhere to this rule by simply playing games of darts in the clubhouse in order to while away the time (currently only another five sleeps away).

The fact that I ask loudly pertinent questions about Noli's financial track record before throwing a dart hard at the manifesto on the board is neither here nor there. You may hear me call: "How many times has the clubs petty cash tin been stolen in the last three years? One hundred and eighty!" is merely the manner in which I warm up for a gentle evening of darts with impressionable young voters who have strayed into the clubhouse.

So, dear and financially accountable and legally liable reader and voter, please feel free to apply your vote to the excellent candidate for our club's Chairmanship on 1 January at the AGM. I wouldn't blame you if you placed your X on the spot that spells out D J O K O V I C H, N. If I didn't have some inside intelligence about various alleged financial irregularities, I would probably have voted for him too.

But if you want a chairman who is going to lead the club to financial security rather than the swamp of litigation, claims and counterclaims following last year's odd use of Lawn Tennis Association funding then I suggest your vote would be most wisely allocated to yours truly, the soon-to-be Lord Andrew John Paul George Ringo Murray of Kirkintilloch (PhD pending).

WHY SERENA WILLIAMS IS NOT GOING TO MAKE IT (6–3)

I am not the type of person who will quibble about the type of person who will apply for a role entitled 'Chairman' when that second type of person is clearly not a man. Neither am I the kind of person who will bleat on about political correctness gone mad, should that second type of person complain about the first kind of person's alleged complaint in an alleged off the cuff alleged remark to a third kind of person: the type of person who takes things much too seriously and who is liable to file a legal action against you should you so much as dare to observe that the second type of person is not like either the first or third kind of person.

This, in a nutshell, is why Mrs. Serena 'Bolshie' Williams is highly unlikely to be voted as Chairman of our venerable club at its AGM this coming pinch-punch first day of the month i.e. January 1, 2014. Not because she is a representative of either the first, second or third type of person identified here.

Oh dear me, no!

Mrs Bolshie Williams isn't any type of person at all, she is a person in her own right and cannot be simplistically labelled as any type of anything.

I'm glad we've cleared that one up.

No, the reason why the tennis giant that is Mrs Serena Bolshie would be a poor choice of Chairman for our club is because she would actually be a great choice as a Deputy Chairman, playing second fiddle to someone who had a greater range of social and political acumen to draw upon; someone who could bring a certain degree of gravitas and level headedness to the club's proceedings; someone exactly like me, perhaps.

Mrs Bolshie and I would, if you like, be the 'dream ticket' for the future leadership of our club. I, the soon-to-be Lord Andy J.P.G.R. Murray of Kirkintilloch would deal with mission, vision and overarching big arm waving conceptual challenges. Mrs Bolshie would be able to deal with the gentler, pinker side of getting things done. Things like cleaning the patio, welcoming visiting rugby teams, and shooing away unwanted guests during the club's car-boot sales.

So, dear voter, you can see that I have the best interests of our club at the centre of my heart in this unprovoked and unilateral offer to the wider membership: vote for me and get Mrs Bolshie as a value added extra. A kind of BOGOF approach to democracy if you like.

Remember, as our good family friend Mr Harold McMillan once remarked to the nation as a whole, some of you have never had it so good.

SHOCK HORROR EARLY EXIT OF NADAL AND WILLIAMS (7–3)

You know something is most definitely afoot in the land of tennis politics when you walk into a bar and heads turn, faces look at you in awe, and a hush descends.

Well, avuncular and fascinated reader, this is exactly what happened at the Club bar last night, just 3 sleeps from the result of the vote for the role of Chairman of our esteemed tennis club.

A mild tittering broke the brief spell but by now I am immune to the barbs and arrows of outrageous teenagers, assorted nay-sayers and quislings.

For my journey is nearly complete: I have the Wimbledon Men's single final urn, the SPOTY gift voucher and – by this time on 1 January – I, the soon-to-be-Lord Andrew John Paul George Ringo Murray of Kirkintilloch shall be adorned with the traditional wreath of tennis netting and shuttlecocks commemorating the achievement of my final quest: the Chairmanship of our august tennis club.

I have it on very good authority that two of my three opponents have withdrawn their interest in the role. Rafa Nadal's lack of any sort of driving licence has ruled him out as the role requires its incumbent to ferry committee members from bar to bar over the course of Wimbledon fortnight in 2014. Dear honourable Rafa realised the game was up when asked to produce his driving licence recently by Jeremy, the club security guard, who had apparently been tipped off about Rafa's intention to borrow the Club tractor and drive it into town after a heavy night on the Hawkeye.

Mrs Serena Bolshie Williams has withdrawn in more mysterious circumstances. One minute her name was on the list pinned on the large club notice board above the faux fireplace; four hours later, by the end of the evening, it had been mysteriously tippexed over – meaning her candidature was now null and void (Club rule Para 418 subsection 1322i).

It was a surprise to all of us I can tell you, myself especially as I was fully expecting to run on a dream ticket with her. But mine is not to reason why. I just hope we will be able to shake hands and look each other in the eye on 1 January once the vote is announced. My first job will be to catch the scoundrel who erased poor Mrs Williams name from the list.

That just leaves me and Novak 'Novi' Djokovic (or Djovak 'Dovi' Nokovich depending on his mental stability at the time) to slug it out. How apt. A re-run of the Wimbledon Men's semi-final of 2013. But instead of facing each other over a tennis net, this time it will be over the ballot box.

Time to resurrect the questions concerning the whereabouts of the funding from the Lawn Tennis Association and the continual disgraceful state of our grass courts methinks.

Life has never felt so good.

LATE BREAKING NEWS FROM THE DAILY RECORD (8–3)

The excitement was at fever pitch down at the Greater Dunblane Tennis Rackets and Cricket Club last night with the imminent vote for the post of Chairman of the Club's Committee. Locals Bert and Agnes Fletcher claimed they had never seen anything like it.

"We've never seen anything like it," they said to our Daily Record reporter, Brian Blessed, amidst scenes which resembled the sales department at the local B and Q on Boxing Day.

"Voting papers were being given out like confetti and little black stubby pencils couldn't be found for love nor money. It was just like Christmas and New Year had come together and were happening within a few days of each other."

The furore is down to a fiercely contested contest between two tennis stars of international repute, our very own much loved Andy Murray (who we believe to be in imminent receipt of a major award from HRH Queen Elizabeth II) and the equally admired yet slightly robotic Novak Djokovich whose prowess on the mixed doubles tennis courts has astounded generations of tennis players both near and far. We caught up with both candidates in the club bar during a lull in the excitement.

"I'm honoured to have been short listed for this prestigious award," beamed Murray whilst simultaneously signing autographs, kissing babies and offering business growth advice to local entrepreneurs. *"I am over-awed that the local community has so much faith in me and would be over the moon to pay back their faith in me. But it's a game of two halves, Brian, and I fully respect Djovak Nokovich's contribution over the many years he has served the club and how he has tended to its finances."*

Novak was equally effusive about Andy and rated the next competition as being one of the hardest he has ever fought.

"Andy is a supreme athlete, astute politician and international statesman whose presence as chairman would grace any tennis club anywhere in the world. Even in my hometown of Obrenovac near Belgrade, we have built a shrine to him for what he has done for Serbian tennis. I fully intend to give my everything to this competition, but Andy is going to be an impossible act to beat."

Voting starts on mid-day 31 December and closes at midday on 1 January. The results will be published at 4pm in time for our evening edition and available online.

THE JEREMY PAXMAN INTERVIEW ON NEWSNIGHT (9–3)

On Monday 30 December Jeremy Paxman interviewed the two leading candidates for the leadership of the Greater Dunblane Cricket, Rackets and Tennis Club, Andrew Murray and Novak Djokovic. Below is a transcript of the programme. This transcript was supplied by an external organisation. The BBC is not responsible for its content.

PAXMAN: Good evening. In the first and only interview with the potential leader of the biggest Lawn Tennis club in British sport, tonight we're talking here in London Docklands to Andrew Murray and Novak Djokovic. You have both been out of power since you went down to your last crashing defeats last year. Now, Andrew Murray, why would anybody want to bring you back in to govern your club?

MURRAY: Because I will take action on the things which matter to the country and the things which matter to people, and that's why I've been spelling out my plans to bring to this club court discipline, clean changing rooms, more security guards, controlled membership, lower bar prices, the things that people really do care about and the things that are important for the club's future and unlike Mr Djokovic who talks a lot but does very little, I will carry out the promises I make.

PAXMAN: Excellent. Now, Novak Djokovic, why would anybody want to bring you back in to govern your club? You were the man who presided over that embarrassing fiasco with the funding from the Lawn Tennis Association.

DJOKOVIC: Urm. Well let's talk about those things. The LTA funding was indeed a terrible mistake. When we went into the LTA, I was supported by the current committee and Mr Murray too and I am the only one that's learned our lesson...

PAXMAN: It's about judgement Mr Djokovic.

DJOKOVIC: No, no – just let me finish. Indeed, it is, it is about judgement. I am the only candidate that's learned our lesson from that.

PAXMAN: We all know what Blairism is, we knew what Thatcherism was. What is Murrayism Mr. Murray?

MURRAY: Murrayism, if you want to use that word, is a practical programme for dealing with the challenges facing this club. For changing the direction of the club and for putting in place things which really matter to ordinary people in their lives. That's why for example, I'm talking today about crime, crime's gone up, crime's out of control, especially crime relating to petty cash tins and funding going missing. People need a chairman that's going to get a grip on the problems facing the club, and I'm spelling out exactly how I'm going to do that.

PAXMAN: Excellent. What is Djokovism, Mr. Djokovic? As you've already conceded, it is a matter of judgement and you've been wrong on so many issues haven't you?

DJOKOVIC: Well I've been er… I've been right on very many issues I – I mean let's talk about it… If you, you want to talk about the past I'm very happy to do so.

PAXMAN: You opposed the national minimum wage being applied to
(overlaps) the Club Security guards. You said it would cost two million jobs. It hasn't has it? You threatened to over-rule the Club Chairman on the issue didn't you?

DJOKOVIC: Well hang on. I, I won't just talk about things. I won't start things and not finish them. I won't pussy foot about, I'll actually do the things I'm promising.

PAXMAN: It hasn't cost two million jobs at the cricket club has it?

DJOKOVIC: And I've learned lessons.

PAXMAN: It didn't cost two million jobs did it?

DJOKOVIC: The truth of the matter is that Jeremy earned more than the minimum wage when you take his bonuses into account.

PAXMAN: It didn't cost two million jobs did it? Didn't you overrule the Chairman on the issue at the finance committee?

DJOKOVIC: I did not overrule the chairman.

PAXMAN: Did you threaten to overrule him?

DJOKOVIC: I took advice on what I could or could not do…

PAXMAN: Did you threaten to overrule him?

DJOKOVIC: and acted scrupulously in accordance with that advice. I did not over-rule the Chairman.

PAXMAN: Did you threaten to over-rule him?

DJOKOVIC: I have accounted for my decision to dismiss the security firm…

PAXMAN: Did you threaten to overrule him?

DJOKOVIC: in great detail before the Club Committee.

PAXMAN: I note that you're not answering the question whether you threatened to over-rule him.

DJOKOVIC: Well, the important aspect of this which it's very clear to bear in mind…

PAXMAN: I'm sorry, I'm going to be frightfully rude but – I'm sorry – it's a straight yes-or-no question and a straight yes-or-no answer: did you threaten to over-rule him?

DJOKOVIC: I discussed the matter with the chairman. I gave him the benefit of my opinion. I gave him the benefit of my opinion in strong language, but I did not instruct him because I was not, er, entitled to instruct him. I was entitled to express my opinion and that is what I did.

PAXMAN: With respect, that is not answering the question of whether you threatened to over-rule him.

DJOKOVIC: It's dealing with the relevant point which was what I was entitled to do and what I was not entitled to do, and I have dealt with this in detail before the relevant committee.

PAXMAN: But with respect you haven't answered the question of whether you threatened to overrule him.

DJOKOVIC: Well, you see, the question is...

PAXMAN: Well, it's good night from him and it's good night from me. Goodnight.

MURRAY: Goodnight.
(Off camera)

PAXMAN: I think you're going to win.
(to Murray)

MURRAY: Thank you Jeremy.

PAXMAN: Novak, that was a very impressive response. I'm well impressed.

DJOKOVIC: Thank you Jeremy. I enjoyed our tussle.

PAXMAN: But you're probably not going to win the chairmanship.

DJOKOVIC: I think you're probably right.

PAXMAN: Where are you lot headed now?

DJOKOVIC: How about the Grafton? It's Grab-a-Granny night.

PAXMAN: Sounds good to me. Do you want to share a cab?

(Indistinct muttering as they all leave the studio).

THANK YOU HRH QE2: THE FUTURE OF SCOTTISH TENNIS HAS NEVER LOOKED BRIGHTER (10–3)

Lord Andrew Murray. Lord Andy Murray. My Lord Andrew of Murray. Milord Murray of Kirkintilloch. Any way you shake it, it fits like a glove.

And yet it's clear that the message never got through to HRH. And I had it on caste-iron authority that a knighthood was in the bag! So much for the Royal Post.

Surely some mistake? I hear you, my devoted reader, mutter to yourself?

Surely that Andy Murray cannot have been overlooked in such a flagrant manner after having won every conceivable major tennis tournament in Christendom? Surely, he deserved something which recognised his contribution to tennis communities from Belize to Bangkok? Surely… Surely… Surely…?

Well, dear devoted reader, let me cool your fevered brow and help you stop your fretting. The fact of the matter is that being spurned by HRH QE2 is actually playing out in my favour in a way I could never have conceived of just twenty-four hours ago.

The phone hasn't stopped ringing since the crack of dawn and the New Year's Honours List was leaked two days before it was supposed to be officially released. I've had actors, academics, film stars, elite sportsmen and the odd politician (naming no names Mr. Salmond!) contact me to express their sympathies for my being locked out of the inn of this year's Honours List.

My rejection by the establishment has actually fuelled the fire of my campaign for the bigger prize of all: the chairmanship of the Greater Dunblane Tennis, Rackets and Cricket Club. All sorts of odd people are falling out of the woodwork to wish me luck tomorrow and to pledge their allegiance against the colonial imperialists of the English Establishment. They see me as their Chairman in waiting and I shall be only too happy to oblige once the votes are added up tomorrow and the announcement made.

Chair-man-ship of the Tennis Club. Say it loud, say it proud, say it like Homer Simpson if you must, say it anyway you like: it just sounds goooooood.

The future of Scottish tennis never looked brighter.

THE LAST POST BEFORE THE BRAND NEW DAWN (11-3)

Sat here in my cravat and boater, sipping a glass or two of Hawkeye Premiere Cru out of my favourite brass flagon, I reflect on what has been a tumultuous year and what is promising to be an even more frenetic 2014.

Because now, dear devoted reader, the voting for the chairmanship of the Greater Dunblane Tennis Rackets and Cricket Club is complete, the counting has begun in earnest and by midday tomorrow, I shall wake up and recover from my revels to find my fate.

Without wishing to tempt aforesaid extra-terrestrial influence, I am confident that my next meeting with the Club Committee will see me being handed the golden key to the stationery cupboard - a symbolic act of the transference of power which will herald the first days of transformative change at the Club which will last the next 25 years. Friends, relatives, acquaintances, complete strangers, Facebook Friends and one-time enemies have all come up to me this afternoon whilst laying prone on the club house floor to assure me of their vote and support. So, the die is cast and now I am in the hands of our excellent electoral system.

So, dear reader, I wish you a very Happy New Year, stay safe on our roads tonight, and prepare for government!

See you on the other side of the equator!

NOTICE OF SUSPENSION OF CLUB MEMBER (0-6, PLAYER DISQUALIFIED)

It has come to the attention of the Greater Dunblane Tennis Club Committee that A. Murray, Esq. has been contravening the rules and regulations of the Club since June 2013 namely:

* Bringing the club into disrepute (Para. 1.14, section 22);

* Lobbying for an official position in the Club's committee when expressly informed not to by a current official (Para 2.44 section 89)

* Making unsubstantiated allegations of criminal activity against other club members (Para 8.02 section 167iii);

* Making insulting and offensive comments about club members in the public bar (Para 33.16 section 533iv);

* Refusing to conduct himself in an orderly fashion when asked to leave the premises (Para 55.25 section 866xix);

* Damaging club property viz. the Club grass tennis courts (Para 117.54 section 1446xxxiv)

* Behaving in an inappropriate manner on other club property viz. urinating on the Club Cricket pitch (Para 242.42 section 3955cxxxix).

As a result of these contraventions, A. Murray, Esq. has been banned from the club, its premises and the use of any of its assets until such time as the committee see fit to reinstate his membership.

He has been instructed by the Club Secretary, Ms Grace Favour to desist from publishing any further inflammatory material whatsoever. Refusal to comply with this instruction will result in legal action against Mr. Murray.

Should you wish to contact him, please do so through the normal channels. This matter is now closed.

Ms Serena Williams,

Chair, Greater Dunblane Tennis Club,

1 January 2014

FIFTH SET:
TIE BREAKER.

(FIRST SET: 2–6)
(SECOND SET: 11–5)
(THIRD SET: 6–3)
(FOURTH SET: 0–6, PLAYER DISQUALIFIED)

THE ALL NEW LIVERPOOL DAILY POST EST ARRIVÉ! STRANGE SIGHTINGS AT OTTERSPOOL PROM (0-1)

The early morning promenaders of Otterspool Promenade in Aigburth, Liverpool, were treated to a grisly sight on their first morning stroll after the festive season - a makeshift funeral pyre floating down the River Mersey.

In scenes reminiscent of gatherings on the Ganges, a small flaming raft was pulled ashore by coast-guards at about 6am on Thursday, 2 January in the vicinity of Riversdale Campus of Liverpool City College. The area was immediately cordoned off by police and a full investigation launched.

Police were unable to confirm whether or not there were any fatalities but described the funeral pyre as consisting of a collection of second-hand burning tennis rackets, a tennis court net and dozens of used tennis balls, the makes of which are still to be confirmed.

Police also confirmed that local tennis clubs were assisting them with their enquiries.

THE ALL NEW LIVERPOOL DAILY POST: NEW YEAR'S FIRES PERPLEX LOCAL FIRE SERVICES IN SOUTH LIVERPOOL (0-2)

South Liverpool fire chiefs and police have been perplexed since 2 January when over fifty large bonfires have been set alight between Speke and Dingle, all of them on the grounds or near to local sports clubs.

While there have been no casualties as yet, police are proceeding on the basis that the fires are the work of a local arsonist who knows the area well enough to be able to get access to the clubs without raising suspicions and that it will only be a matter of time before some serious injury is reported.

In a statement, Chief Inspector Murray said:

"Even more bizarrely, the fires tend to consist of used sports equipment such as tennis rackets, cricket bats, hockey sticks, rugby boots and other assorted items. We ask the public to keep vigilant and remove any old sports equipment from garden sheds or other outhouses which could attract the attention of the suspected arsonist."

Do you have any photos or CCTV footage that might aid the police? If so, please contact the news desk at the All New Liverpool Daily Post and we will pass it on to the relevant authorities.

THE ALL NEW LIVERPOOL DAILY POST: MYSTERY ARSONIST FOUND HIDING ON ALLOTMENT (0-3)

The search into the cause of the mysterious fires around South Liverpool Sports Centres was finally brought to a halt tonight when a middle aged balding Caucasian man wearing nothing but a Fred Perry singlet and a John McEnroe head band was found in an allotment shed sat on a makeshift throne of wooden tennis rackets.

Identifying himself only as Lord Andrew Murray of Kirkintilloch (a small town in East Dunbartonshire, Scotland – editors' note) police stated that the man denied any knowledge of the recent arson attacks in the neighborhood but could not account for the 79 plastic petrol containers which lined the shed's walls and the oxy-acetylene torch which lay idle on the floor.

Mr. Murray – whose real identity is still subject to confirmation – is now helping police with their enquiries and is expected to appear on court in Melbourne for the Australian Open early next month and in court in Liverpool early next week to face charges.

Liverpool Social Services and the Lawn Tennis Association have been informed of the man's arrest.

FINAL
SCORE.

(FIRST SET: 2–6)
(SECOND SET: 11–5)
(THIRD SET: 6–3)
(FOURTH SET: 0–6)
(FIFTH SET: 0–3, PLAYER RETIRED HURT)

ABOUT THE AUTHOR

Nick Owen was awarded an MBE for services to arts-based businesses in 2012 and is passionate about generating culturally inspiring and socially engaging creative practice within educational contexts both nationally and internationally.

He has worked in the creative and cultural industries across the public, private and social enterprise sectors in the East Midlands, Merseyside and Cumbria whilst committed to developing international links with partners in Bulgaria, Chile, India and Serbia amongst others. Honorary Professor of the Faculty of Education at the University of Nottingham, he also serves as Governor of Coventry University. In his spare time he is a keen cyclist, tennis player, fiction writer and Vinyl DJ.

Recent publications include:

Owen, N., Grindley L. and Fujii, M. (2016) Creative Development in The Early Years Foundation Stage: Theory and Practice (1str, 2nd and 3rd Editions, ed. Palaiologou, I.) London: SAGE.

Russell, L. and Owen, N. (2013) The Creative Research Process: Delights and Difficulties. LEARNing

Landscapes, Autumn 2012 Vol.6 No.1 - Creativity: Insights, Directions and Possibilities. Québec: LEARN.

Owen, N. (2011) Placing Students at the Heart of Creative Learning (Series Editors: Sefton-Green, J. Ruthra-Rajan, N. and Thomson, P.) London: Routledge.

Owen, N. (2011) Outsider | Insiders: becoming a creative partner with schools International Handbook of Creative Learning, (Eds. Sefton Green, J., Thomson P., Bresler, L. and Jones, K). London: Routledge.

Owen, N. and Munden, P. (2010) Class Writing York: National Association of Writers in Education.

Owen, N. (2010) Closing Schools for the Future. Proceedings of the 1st International Conference on Educational Research for Development, Vol. 1. Ethiopia: Addis Ababa University.

Owen, N. (2007) When Herbert Met Ken: Understanding the 100 Languages of Creativity English in Education / National Association for the Teaching of English, Vol. 41 No. 2.

Planning for Creative Development in The Early Years Foundation Stage: Theory and Practice. (Ed. Palaiologou, I.) London: SAGE (2009).

ABOUT THE ILLUSTRATOR

"I've always, as far back as I can remember, sketched and drawn and painted images.

I attended the Joseph Wright Secondary Art School in Derby but didn't follow that with art college and an arts-based career. I drifted through a range of full-time jobs including the army, the building trade, milk delivery, postal delivery and counter work and architectural office assistance to name but several.

In 2013, after renting studio space at Harington Mill Studios in Long Eaton, I began drawing on an iPad and I have drawn on an iPad ever since. My drawing style is continually evolving and developing. I draw people, the human figure and add a sprinkling of artistic license. I don't strictly create pictures; I'm interested in facial expression, stance, form, interaction between members of society, a moment in the workaday activities. Spending a great deal of time drawing, daily, weekly, I produce many digital images, some of which go on to be printed, mounted, framed and, from time to time, exhibited.

If asked how to best describe my imagery, I'd say it is figurative "momentism," attempting a drawing that represents a male or female, or both, in a moment that was there a moment ago and is now gone." **Paul Warren, Long Eaton, April 2021.**

"This is a riotous, rolling, rollicking read in the picaresque tradition. Eat your hearts out Henry Fielding and Herman Melville. As the hero hurtles through his ruthless pursuit of fame and glory, you too will probably receive an upgrade as you are laughing so much in your plane or train seat. Witty (and wise) this is a cracking read. First in a series." **Liz Fincham, writer.**

"I am at the ageing tennis player age and this book hits the nail on the head with an insight and humour that made me laugh out loud. Great observation, no holds barred honesty through the arena of tennis that explores between our imagination and the actuality." **Mike Stubbs, artist, curator, consultant.**

9 780956 142337

"A rollicking good read that had me laughing out loud. It had me entertaining the idea of joining our local tennis club, and I'm rubbish at tennis." **The Shed**

Printed in Great Britain
by Amazon

50812090R00066